FEARLESS

How a diagnosis of a chronic disease turned my world upside down.

JO ANN MAXWELL

WestBow
PRESS®
A DIVISION OF THOMAS NELSON
& ZONDERVAN

Scripture taken from the New King James Version. Copyright © 1979, 1980,
1982 by Thomas Nelson, Inc. Used by permission. All rights reserved.

This book is a work of non-fiction. Unless otherwise noted, the author
and the publisher make no explicit guarantees as to the accuracy of
the information contained in this book and in some cases, names of
people and places have been altered to protect their privacy.

WestBow Press books may be ordered through booksellers or by contacting:

WestBow Press
A Division of Thomas Nelson & Zondervan
1663 Liberty Drive
Bloomington, IN 47403
www.westbowpress.com
1 (866) 928-1240

Because of the dynamic nature of the Internet, any web addresses or
links contained in this book may have changed since publication and
may no longer be valid. The views expressed in this work are solely those
of the author and do not necessarily reflect the views of the publisher,
and the publisher hereby disclaims any responsibility for them.

Any people depicted in stock imagery provided by Thinkstock are models,
and such images are being used for illustrative purposes only.
Certain stock imagery © Thinkstock.

ISBN: 978-1-5127-5372-1 (sc)
ISBN: 978-1-5127-5373-8 (hc)
ISBN: 978-1-5127-5371-4 (e)

Library of Congress Control Number: 2016913638

Print information available on the last page.

WestBow Press rev. date: 9/22/2016

To my God, my Abba Father, and His Son,
Jesus Christ, my Savior and Lord,
and to Holy Spirit, Who flows through me like a Living River.

To my children, whom I love with a love that knows no bounds.
You are my inspiration and my joy!

Psalm 19

The Perfect Revelation of the Lord

To the Chief Musician. A Psalm of David.

The heavens declare the glory of God;
And the firmament shows His handiwork.
Day unto day utters speech,
And night unto night reveals knowledge.
There is no speech nor language
Where their voice is not heard.
Their line has gone out through all the earth,
And their words to the end of the world.
In them He has set a tabernacle for the sun,
Which is like a bridegroom coming out of his chamber,
And rejoices like a strong man to run its race.
Its rising is from one end of heaven,
And its circuit to the other end;
And there is nothing hidden from its heat.

The law of the Lord is perfect, converting the soul;
The testimony of the Lord is sure, making wise the simple;
The statutes of the Lord are right, rejoicing the heart;
The commandment of the Lord is pure, enlightening the eyes;
The fear of the Lord is clean, enduring forever;
The judgments of the Lord are true and righteous altogether.
More to be desired are they than gold,
Yea, than much fine gold;
Sweeter also than honey and the honeycomb.

Moreover by them Your servant is warned,
And in keeping them there is great reward.

Who can understand his errors?
Cleanse me from secret faults.
Keep back Your servant also from presumptuous sins;
Let them not have dominion over me.
Then I shall be blameless,
And I shall be innocent of great transgression.

Let the words of my mouth and the meditation of my heart
Be acceptable in Your sight,
O LORD, my strength and my Redeemer.

CONTENTS

FOREWORD

I have MS, and Jo Ann has MS; this chronic disease brought us together. We share common interests and careers that required a passion that enables us to serve others, and this forged us as friends. We believe that Jesus, the Son of God, is our Savior, and we live to praise Him and serve as He guides.

I met Jo Ann in 2012 at TACID, Tacoma Area Coalition of Individuals with Disabilities. She was the Deputy Executive Director. She joined the Tacoma MS self-help group, which met at TACID. I invited her to also join a smaller, less-formal support group, which I called Girl Bonding. I organized it with several women from different backgrounds and ages, and all with a chronic neurological disease that changed life as they previously knew it. We met together once a month over lunch at a lovely small cafe, just having a good time over lunch and girl talk.

We decided to learn more about the symptoms we shared and ways they could be treated. We also helped each other problem solve issues, some personal, and answer questions, trading tips and giving advice for all. We talked often about how to accept and create our own "new normal" in our lives. We agreed this meant keeping on meaningful paths that included new goals and support. We affirmed that support could come in many different forms, including a spiritual life. Even though we had different thoughts about who God is, or who our higher power is, we came together in love and mutual edification. We supported each other, knowing that spirituality is very important to our well-being.

Jo Ann and I got to know each other better and shared how faith in our lives was helping us deal with some of the many things MS had brought into our lives. We also learned we shared a passion for ice cream. We visited Cold Stone Creamery to get some of the best ice cream, and we often had conversations about blessings.

Since she moved to North Carolina, Jo Ann and I keep in touch. We have had many wonderful hours on the phone chatting about our faith, trials, and blessings too. We both draw on God's strength in our weaknesses and try to remember to thank Him for both blessings and trials, though we note that thanks for the trials are not easy.

We noted a lack of any mention of faith and spirituality in materials about MS, so we thought that a blog or an article would be good for others to hear how we rely on our faith and how it helps provide us support, guidance, even courage. Eventually she started talking about a book discussing the many facets of the disease and how faith does and can enable us to keep going forward every day. She is now like others, who write about their own journeys, wishing to help others who come after. Her journey is with MS and how she has relied on faith and her spiritual life to help herself and others. This kind of sharing is what I call "pay it forward" wisdom and service.

Linda M. Moran
MS Activist
Senior Assistant Attorney General, State of Washington, retired

INTRODUCTION

I love to pray. Actually, I can't help but pray. It is an obsession with me. God says in Ezekiel 22:30, "So I sought for a man among them who would make a wall, and stand in the gap before Me on behalf of the land, that I should not destroy it; but I found no one." I long to be that person standing in the gap for my family, friends, church, and nation. Jesus prayed with loud cries and tears to His Father. If Jesus prayed with loud cries and tears, I can do no less.

The prayers in this book are all based on God's Word. I believe all Scripture is "God-breathed and is useful for teaching, rebuking, correcting and training in righteousness, so that I may be thoroughly equipped for every good work."[1] I believe in each and every Scripture—not just those I like.

Why do I believe in the Bible? First of all, because the Holy Spirit in me testifies that it is the truth. It was written over a period of sixteen hundred years, it was written by forty different men, over 168,000 copies are sold or given away every day, and it has been translated into more that twelve hundred languages. There are seven hundred prophecies in the Old Testament that Jesus fulfilled in the New Testament, and it does not contradict itself from beginning to end. From Genesis 1:1 to Revelation 22:21, the

Bible can be summed up by, "For God so loved the world that He gave His only begotten Son, that whoever believes in Him should not perish but have everlasting life. For God did not send His Son into the world to condemn the world, but that the world through Him might be saved."[2]

I believe that praying God's Word is a way to pray in line with His will. Jesus told His disciples, "For your Father knows the things you have need of before you ask Him. In this manner, therefore, pray: Our Father in heaven, Hallowed be Your name. Your kingdom come. Your will be done."[3] He also says: "If anyone wills to do His will, he shall know concerning the doctrine, whether it is from God or whether I speak on My own authority."[4] In other words, seek the Scriptures (doctrine) to find out what God's will is.

As an example of how I pray God's Word and make it my own, I'll use Psalm 91.

> I dwell in the secret place of the Most High and
> Shall abide under the shadow of the Almighty.
> I will say of the LORD, "You are my refuge and
> my fortress;
> My God, in You I will trust."
>
> Surely You will deliver me from the snare of the
> fowler
> And from the perilous pestilence.
> You shall cover me with Your feathers,
> And under Your wings I will take refuge;
> Your truth shall be my shield and buckler.

I shall not be afraid of the terror by night,
Nor of the arrow that flies by day,
Nor of the pestilence that walks in darkness,
Nor of the destruction that lays waste at noonday.

A thousand may fall at my side,
And ten thousand at my right hand;
But it shall not come near me.
Only with my eyes shall I look,
And see the reward of the wicked.

Because I have made the LORD, who is my refuge,
Even the Most High, my dwelling place,
No evil shall befall me,
Nor shall any plague come near my dwelling;
For You shall give Your angels charge over me,
To keep me in all my ways.

In their hands they shall bear me up,
Lest I dash my foot against a stone.
I shall tread upon the lion and the cobra,
The young lion and the serpent I shall trample
underfoot.

Because I have set my love upon You, therefore
You will deliver me;
You will set me on high, because I have known
Your name.
I shall call upon You, and You will answer me;
You will be with me in trouble;
You will deliver me and honor me.
With long life You will satisfy me,
And show me Your salvation.

I took a Bible study several years ago called the "Names of God." I have learned to rely on His different names ("Hallowed be Your name") at different times of my life. To know His names is to know His character. To know His character is to know and understand the depths of His love. So I rely on His names as I pray.

It is my hope and prayer that not only people with MS or those who love someone with MS but also those with other serious long-term chronic diseases will find hope in these pages. I pray these pages will be an encouragement to all of you. I pray for the Holy Spirit to teach me in what I ought to say (Luke 12:12). I pray my journey back to fearlessness will give you tools to use in your own lives. My story is not like your story, but we all are in need of hope in our lives. That hope can only be found in Jesus Christ.

God bless you each of you. May the grace, peace, and hope of Jesus Christ be with you always.

Jo Ann Maxwell
fearlessinJesusChrist.blogspotcom
fearlessinJesusChrist@gmail.com

LIFE BEFORE MS

I will praise you, for I am fearfully and wonderfully made; marvelous are your works, and that my soul knows very well. (Psalm 139:14)

I was fearless. I had the world by the tail. I knew what I wanted and went after it. I was successful and felt good about my life.

I was an athlete in an athletic family. I participated in age-group AAU swimming from ages eight to seventeen. I traveled extensively throughout the Midwest and swam both long course (fifty-meter pools) and short course (twenty-five-yard pools). I was most successful in the short course meets as it was in twenty-five-yard pools in which I trained. While in high school, I trained with the local college men's team and was faster than at least half of the men! I was very excited when I became a Junior Olympic champion in the hundred-yard free. After my age-group experience, I then swam in college from ages eighteen to nineteen. I was blessed to compete at the collegiate nationals as a freshman in Tempe, Arizona. I was a sprinter, swimming mostly freestyle and backstroke. I swam some Individual Medley races (swimming butterfly, backstroke, breaststroke, and freestyle consecutively in one race) but didn't like those races as much as I had a weak breaststroke.

I am the middle girl between two boys, so I was a tomboy. We grew up playing games of hide and seek after dark throughout the summer, jumping off bridges at the local golf course into leaves we would rake up in the fall, and sledding and skating in the winter. This was before any thoughts of personal computers, and we spent our time when not in school out of doors.

We were all Scouts and loved camping as Scouts and with just our family. I became a Brownie in first grade and continued through elementary school and then through high school. I loved selling Girl Scout cookies and was the selling champion from our troop, using a red flyer wagon loaded to overflowing as I delivered cookies throughout our neighborhood. I became a camp counselor through high school and loved teaching and mentoring the younger scouts.

As a family, my favorite camping trip was to the Rocky National Park just west of Estes Park, Colorado. This trip was life changing for me as I fell in love with Colorado. I loved the cool nights and glorious days of cerulean sky and no humidity.

My dad was a college professor and track coach, and my mom taught fourth grade. Everywhere we traveled we took "school teacher tours." We always had to attend the park ranger talks, go to the museums, and learn all about the flora, fauna, animals, and rock or land formations. (Of course, I did the same with my kids!) I grew up in the '50s and '60s and had a fairly sheltered, easy life. We grew up safe and innocent. I come from hardy Anglo-Saxon heritage who believe in hard work and lots of gumption.

I knew I was going to be a teacher when I was twelve. In high school, my mother thought I should teach math, as I was very good at all levels of anything related to numbers. I told her I wanted to have fun in my job, as I thought math was pretty boring. I began teaching swimming to younger kids at age fourteen. I received my WSI (Water Safety Instructor) certificate at eighteen. I lifeguarded and taught swimming every summer through college.

I went to the University of Northern Colorado for my bachelor's degree, married, started my career, and had two awesome kids. They are now thirty-seven and thirty-five. I have two amazing granddaughters, aged nine and five. Being a grandparent is the best job in the world! My children endured a difficult process of growing up. Their dad died when they were young. I was single for seven years, then married a wolf in sheep's clothing. It was disastrous for all of us. My kids are strong and confident despite the difficulties. I am so proud of them! My son is an amazing dad to his two girls. My daughter loves being an aunt, and they have great adventures together! They are both successful professionally.

As the kids were growing up, we were active in many ways, including sports, travel, and scouting. We traveled extensively, and they have visited more than 75 percent of the continental forty-eight states. We've been to Disneyland and Disney World. We spent a lot of time in Breckenridge, Colorado, during summer vacations. I would do most of my Christmas shopping there and usually had it completed during our summer breaks. I have traveled to Mexico, Canada, India, and Norway for the 1994 Winter Olympics with my great friends who live in Colorado.

I taught physical education to elementary through high school children and taught and coached kids K–12 who had physical and mental disabilities. The last seven years of teaching, I organized a Special Olympics program for our school district. We had over one hundred athletes and participated in seven sports. I was blessed to have eight assistant coaches, most of whom I am still good friends with today. Many of our athletes competed and excelled at the 1991 World Summer Games in St. Paul, Minnesota.

I had a friendly wager with another area coach that my power lifter would place better than his. Of course, mine turned out to be the better man!

I was so passionate about Special Olympics that I left teaching to work for Special Olympics Montana full time. I love the athletes' innocence and joy. They have no pretension and love learning. I moved myself and my two teenaged kids to Montana, not knowing anyone in the state. Looking back on that move, I marvel at the fearlessness I felt. I recruited and trained over 250 local area coaches and organized four multisport statewide competitions throughout Montana. While there, I led our delegation to the 1995 World Summer Games in New Haven, Connecticut.

The Special Olympics World Games are fashioned after the Olympics. We had an athletes' village, special programs such as a dance, entertainers throughout all of the multiple venues, grand award ceremonies, and spectacular Opening and Closing Ceremonies, complete with parades of the athletes. It was a blessing and pure joy to be a part of two of them.

Through various vocational and locale changes, I was blessed to open a newly built Boys & Girls Club (BGC) in beautiful Gig Harbor, Washington. We began a fruitful collaboration with the Gig Harbor Schools, as well as other local businesses and local residents who were also large gift donors. After an organizational restructuring at BGC, I became the Deputy Executive Director at a nonprofit specializing in services to adults with disabilities. I was laid off from that position and went on unemployment for the first time in thirty-nine years of working. It was quite a shock. But God had other plans for me.

As I was applying to job after job, I started to sense God wanted me to move to North Carolina and assist my aging parents. I told God no. I wanted to find a good job and stay where my kids and grandkids lived. He told me, "No, I want you to help your parents in North Carolina." We went around the burning bush a couple of times until I realized He was orchestrating my life, not me. His thoughts are higher than mine. (Isaiah 55:8–9 says, "'For My thoughts are not your thoughts, nor are your ways My ways,' says the LORD. 'For as the heavens are higher than the earth, so are My ways higher than your ways, and My thoughts than your thoughts.'") My dad was dealing with COPD and was on oxygen 24/7. When I arrived in July, he could still go out for a shopping or dining experience. By January 2015, he was put on in-home hospice, and in March 2015, he passed away. I continue to provide support and companionship to my mother, which she is thankful for.

Along the way I have made some amazing friends, who stand beside me through thick and thin. They are lifelong friends, and we love connecting through the various means technology has afforded, but face-to-face is always best, albeit rarely. They are in Colorado, Nebraska, Montana, and Washington. You know who you are—and I love you all!

I was sixty years old when I received the diagnosis of Multiple Sclerosis. About two years prior to that, I began experiencing some mobility and hand weakness problems. The doctor I was seeing did not see the need for further testing. When I changed insurance companies in January 2012, I scheduled an appointment with a new physical therapist. She told me that she couldn't help me until I had my hip looked at by an orthopedist. Eventually, I received notice that I needed my hip replaced. So, silly me, I thought all my troubles would be over.

After the hip replacement in October 2012, all of the leg, foot (foot drop), and hand weakness remained. Several MRIs later showed that I had MS. That came on January 4, 2013. My world spun off into a new trajectory. I was shocked, relieved, devastated, and fearful of what my future would look like.

My neurologist thinks I have had MS for at least thirty years. As I learn all I can about this disease, I realize that there were moments that symptoms began and were explained away by other reasons. More about that in the next chapter.

Suggested Prayer

Father God, You are Jehovah Jireh, the One who provides.[1] As you did for Abraham, You have provided for me throughout my life. I have had a wonderful upbringing and opportunities to use the gifts You have given me. I thank You with all my heart and praise Your Holy name. May You bless my friends and family who have been such a blessing to me. And Father, for those reading these pages who do not have the support from friends and/or family as I have, I pray that You would bless them with godly friends to come into their lives. "You are worthy, O Lord, To receive glory and honor and power; For you created all things, and by your will they exist and were created."[2] In Jesus name, Amen.

Personal Reflection

Have you ever felt fearless? Describe what that felt like for you.

Describe your childhood and growing up. What are some key moments that you look back on that you have happy memories for?

Whether your parents are still living or have passed away, how would you describe your relationship with them?

Were you involved in music or sports or other activities outside of school? What were those and how did they enrich your life?

Describe your education and how you felt about it. Did you go to a trade school, community college, or four year college? You may have started working right after high school. How did you make that decision or did your circumstances make the decision for you?

Describe your work history. Have you found something to do that you are passionate about? Or do you just work to get a paycheck?

Describe a major life change that you may have had. What helped you work through that situation? Was it friends, family, or even strangers?

Have you ever been misdiagnosed? What were the circumstances surrounding this and have you gotten any satisfaction with a diagnosis? If you are still working through that process what kind of support system do you have? Or do you need to reach out to family and friends to be that support system?

Write out a prayer that you would like to lift up to the Lord. Thank him for what he has done and what he will do in your life.

ENTER MS

Trust in the Lord with all your heart, and lean not
on your own understanding. (Proverbs 3:5)

Enter MS. Enter fear. Leading up to the diagnosis, I experienced several symptoms that were explained away by other conditions for three decades.

- Balance—Experiencing balance issues was the first time, I noticed something that didn't seem right. My primary care physician said I was just getting older—at thirty-five! Hmm, I lost all respect for him right then. As long as I can remember I have been clumsy, like a fish out of water. If there was anything to stub my toe on or bump into, I would do it, especially when I would tell myself to miss the obstacle. I find bruises periodically that I don't know where they came from—I probably bumped into something!

- Ringing in my ears—I went to an orthodontist who specialized in TMJ (temporomandibular joint disorder). After braces and $5,000 later, I was still experiencing ringing. I started going to a chiropractor at this time, at the suggestion of the orthodontist. Again, the ringing persisted.

- Falling—I began falling down quite frequently about eleven to twelve years ago for no apparent reason. I experienced a very short blackout period (maybe two to four seconds). I had a neurologist at that time (with a straight face) tell me I had falling down syndrome. Now I don't know if that is real or not, but it sounded pretty suspect to me.

- Inflammation—I had several chiropractors tell me that I had a lot of arthritis in my spine and inflammation. I assumed they knew what they were talking about and took it in stride. I almost felt like it was my fault but wasn't sure how that could be.

- Weakness in hand and foot and foot drop—again, a chiropractor said I just needed more adjustments.
- Incontinence—I kept that to myself until I realized there might be a reason and help for it.
- Cognitive—My memory is spotty, especially for people's names. I also have a hard time finding the right words. I laughed it off and called it my Swiss cheese brain.

So after the hip replacement surgery, the leg and arm weaknesses were still there. Subconsciously I knew it wouldn't improve. But remember, I was fearless. I met life head on, as if it was something to be conquered. I took injuries or stiffness and soreness as normal and I just had to work through it. There couldn't be anything "wrong" with me. But subsequent tests showed I had MS. I had several MRIs of my neck and brain and with and without contrast. First I was relieved that I wasn't going crazy, then I was mad, then I became fearful. And the fear is where my struggle lies.

The National Multiple Sclerosis Society (NMSS) was my first and continues to be my go-to source for information. According to NMSS, Multiple Sclerosis (MS) involves an immune-mediated process in which an abnormal response of the body's immune system is directed against the central nervous system (CNS), which is made up of the brain, spinal cord, and optic nerves. The exact antigen—or target that the immune cells are sensitized to attack—remains unknown, which is why MS is considered by many experts to be "immune-mediated" rather than "autoimmune."

- Within the CNS, the immune system attacks myelin—the fatty substance that surrounds and insulates the nerve fibers—as well as the nerve fibers themselves.

- The damaged myelin forms scar tissue (sclerosis), which gives the disease its name.
- When any part of the myelin sheath or nerve fiber is damaged or destroyed, nerve impulses traveling to and from the brain and spinal cord are distorted or interrupted, producing a wide variety of symptoms.
- The disease is thought to be triggered in a genetically susceptible individual by a combination of one or more environmental factors.
- People with MS typically experience one of four disease courses, which can be mild, moderate or severe.[1]

Relapsing-remitting MS (RRMS)

- RRMS—the most common disease course—is characterized by clearly defined attacks of worsening neurologic function. These attacks—also called relapses, flare-ups or exacerbations—are followed by partial or complete recovery periods (remissions), during which symptoms improve partially or completely and there is no apparent progression of disease. Approximately 85 percent of people with MS are initially diagnosed with relapsing-remitting MS.

Secondary-progressive MS (SPMS)

- The name for this course comes from the fact that it follows after the relapsing-remitting course. Most people who are initially diagnosed with RRMS will eventually transition to SPMS, which means that the disease will begin to progress more steadily (although not necessarily more quickly), with or without relapses. (This is where my disease is at present.)

Primary-progressive MS (PPMS)

- PPMS is characterized by steadily worsening neurologic function from the beginning. Although the rate of progression may vary over time with occasional plateaus and temporary, minor improvements, there are no distinct relapses or remissions. About 10 percent of people with MS are diagnosed with PPMS.

Progressive-relapsing MS (PRMS)

- PRMS—the least common of the four disease courses— is characterized by steadily progressing disease from the beginning and occasional exacerbations along the way. People with this form of MS may or may not experience some recovery following these attacks; the disease continues to progress without remissions.[2]

While the cause (etiology) of MS is still not known, scientists believe that the interaction of several different factors may be involved. To answer this important question, studies are ongoing in the areas of immunology (the science of the body's immune system), epidemiology (the study of patterns of disease in the population), and genetics. Scientists are also studying infectious agents that may play a role. Understanding what causes MS will speed the process of finding more effective ways to treat it and— ultimately—cure it, or even prevent it from occurring in the first place.

In MS, an abnormal immune-mediated response attacks the myelin coating around nerve fibers in the central nervous system, as well as the nerve fibers themselves. In recent years, researchers have been able to identify which immune cells are mounting the attack, some of the factors that cause them to attack, and some of the sites (receptors) on the attacking cells that appear to be attracted to the myelin to begin the destructive process. Ongoing efforts to learn more about the immune-mediated process in MS—what sets it in motion, how it works, and how to slow or stop it—are bringing us closer to understanding the cause of MS.[3]

I had experienced some depression prior to the diagnosis because of the lack of mobility. I loved to walk two to three miles every morning. I also saw changes in my ability to swim. When I couldn't swim and walk as I used to, I was devastated, especially not knowing why. Walking involved tripping and stumbling. I could not perform a whip kick anymore (for breaststroke), and my arm flailed around instead of a nice, straight recovery and strong stroke for backstroke. When I swam freestyle, I experienced similar issues with my right arm. But I wasn't swimming a lot then, so again, I ignored the signs, as I felt confident that the doctors were right that there was nothing "wrong."

I love playing with my granddaughters, but I couldn't get on the floor and play with them or run and play outside! Walking through a zoo was not only fatiguing, but walking was difficult. It was difficult walking through airports. My son told me on several occasions that I couldn't walk in a straight line. With the diagnosis, I sank further into depression and grief. How could I not do the things I loved—and never again—because there is no cure for MS!

As I began telling friends, family, and colleagues, invariably they said, "Oh I am so sorry," or "You look so normal. How can you have a problem?" Please take it from me, those are wrong reactions! Instead, let's make lemonade from these lemons, or in other words, let's support each other in learning how to make the best of a new way of living. Linda Moran, who wrote the foreword, suggested I start a "MS board of directors." As a senior level nonprofit executive, I knew what that meant, and it sounded like a good thing to do. A nonprofit board of directors is a group of like-minded professionals and other passionate local leaders who have the responsibility to the nonprofit to ensure that it is administered appropriately and according to US laws.

I gathered together close friends and family for a meeting. They agreed to assist, but when I moved to North Carolina to be a caregiver for my parents, this was put on the back burner. I suggest anyone with a serious illness to gather a team of health professionals and family and friends you trust to be your support system and you can call on at a moment's notice.

My orthopedic surgeon told me that it would take a year to recover fully from the hip surgery. I scoffed at that because I was going to bounce back fast and was determined to do so. I am always full speed ahead and competitive enough to say, "I'll do it faster." I am by nature positive and upbeat and often have a difficult time with negativity and the "poor me" attitude.

Little did I know that he was right, plus the MS combined to slow down the recovery even more. I have worked with a couple of great physical therapists, and my recovery was steady and sure. I saw milestones reached, and it felt great. They also helped me to see how I can slow down, change some techniques, and still find success.

Some of the strategies I use are:
- I started taking notes for meetings and writing my grocery and to-do lists on my tablet and smartphone since writing is difficult and fatiguing. I still write with my right hand, but I make sure I use fat pens with rubber finger grips. I have to use my whole arm to write, but it seems to work. I

recently received a new iPad Air from my wonderful older brother. It has voice recognition capability for many of the apps. It is so wonderful!

• Eating with my left hand was an interesting transition. I got more on myself and the floor than in my mouth for a week or so. I use steak knives often as I don't have the strength to use a table knife. It takes my whole arm to cut anything.

• I have switched to putting on my makeup with my left hand. But I still use my right hand to apply my mascara. I think if I tried to use my non-dominant hand, I would poke my eye out!

• I am patient with myself (most of the time) when I make typing mistakes. Typing is also very fatiguing, and I put in a lot of extra Is". So if you fiiiiind more Is than necessary, Ii apologiiize up front! I use a roller ball type of moiuse and use my left hand for all moiuse activities. Using my right hand with a traditionial mouse proived toi be very diffiicult.

• I am walking slower and concentrating more on each step. Any incline makes it incredibly difficult, especially going down. I use a cane for long distances or when I am in unsure/in new environments. I have an AFO (ankle foot orthotic) that I can wear, but I found out pretty quickly I can't drive with it. I was leaving a friend's house and my foot got stuck on the accelerator as I was reversing and I took out one of her fences. I couldn't figure out why I wasn't stopping as I thought my foot was on the brake, and I began to push harder. Finally I shifted into drive and left ruts in her gravel driveway. I am just glad I didn't kill any of her chickens! So now I don't drive with it. If I am going to a large store, I put the AFO on before entering and take it off after leaving the store.

- I also can't walk and do other tasks at the same time. If you are walking with me and we need to talk, I have to stop. I guess my brain can only handle one thing at a time. Perhaps language takes priority. I can't fish out my keys or sunglasses from my purse while walking either, so again, I have to stop.
- I used to be the queen of multitasking. I could think of several things at a time and prioritize without lists and reminders. Technology has really helped me in this regard.
- I would load up my hands with as much as I could when I was emptying the dishwasher or readying up the house so I wouldn't have to make so many trips. Now I can hardly carry one thing at a time with my right hand. So I take my time and be smart about holding and carrying things.
- Balance is still an issue, especially in small spaces. If I have to turn around or maneuver within small spaces, my balance is taxed to the max. I am glad when there are walls and furniture to hold on to. There is a T-shirt that says: "I'm not drunk I have MS." I think I would like my balance issues to be because of drinking. Then when I stopped drinking I would be able to walk well!
- Incontinence is an embarrassing issue, and I certainly didn't announce it to the world or my doctor for quite some time. Again, I stood on self-reliance and internal grit. Getting on and off toilets can definitely be a struggle with my right side weakness. So I am glad when I find a toilet that is higher than normal. I am tall (over five-foot-ten), and it can be a long way down and back up. And just making it to the bathroom has its challenges. I try to

read or type one more paragraph, watch TV to the next commercial, or just try to ignore the urge. But I have to be very cognizant of my bladder because the muscle control just isn't there, especially in the middle of the night when I am half asleep and have trouble walking, let alone trying to control my bladder. I am taking a medication now that helps tremendously.

- While I was still working, I wore slacks with a flat front and side zipper. I had started taking an antidepressant, which was supposed to help with my neuropathy pain. Well, it worked, but I gained fifteen pounds (before finally stopping the medication). So think of a weak right hand, a side zipper, weight gain, and trying to hold off going to the toilet as long as possible. It was a perfect storm for an accident. Then if another woman came into the bathroom and wanted to talk! It was not a pretty sight. Good thing I had taken precautions with wearing panty liners!

- Cognitive changes are also tough to admit. I tend to see the cognitive changes as a negative impact on my IQ, thereby causing others to think I am unintelligent. That has been proven by medical professionals to not be the case. (I really have to get over myself!) I have tried to cover up my memory issues of retaining and retrieving new information by saying something I thought was right, and often it is not. I have difficulty with attention and concentration in large/loud situations. I prefer small gatherings. I explain away my lack of verbal fluency as having "brain freeze" or a Swiss cheese brain. However, I need to be honest and state that I just don't remember something.

- Cruise control is the best invention (I started driving at a time when cruise control was not widely available). I love to go fast, and with foot drop on my right side, that is way too easy to accomplish. So I use cruise control on the highway and have also begun to use it while on town streets when there is a large portion of road without stoplights. It's tough to use in high-traffic areas and with lots of stoplights, but cruise control helps me not get so fatigued while I drive. I am probably looking at hand controls in the future.

- Medications for various symptoms can help. I take a bladder control medication that has been a life saver for me. I take an extended release version, and it works very well. I also take a muscle relaxant for my spasms and cramping. It works extremely well. I am looking forward to when the extended release is approved by the FDA.

- I also take a medication for fatigue. I can't really tell a difference when I take it, but I can definitely tell a difference if I don't take it. I am also taking an anti-depressant to help with neuropathic pain.

- I have started a new medication called Ampyra. This is not a disease modifying treatment. It is a symptom-based treatment that is designed to improve walking. It strengthens nerve signals in the muscles to coordinate walking as well as other muscle groups. I am praying for great results!

- Supplements can be very helpful as well. In the past I have spent hundreds of dollars on multivitamin packs. Right now I just take vitamin D and calcium. A lack of vitamin D has been shown to affect the onset of MS.

- I also drink apple cider vinegar diluted in water every morning. The benefits are numerous, but I started taking it to control acid reflux I was experiencing as a side effect of one of my medications. I take the variety that has the "mother" in it. It is more expensive, but it doesn't burn so much going down.

- I haven't talked about bowel issues, but I have tried just about every over the counter stool softener/laxative known to man. Now I am taking psyllium tables daily, and those seem to help me the best. I take Acidophilus for general gut health.
- I have known about aromatherapy for some time, but never really thought it was useful. Recently a friend introduced me to lavender for sore and tense muscles and joint pain (as well as many other benefits) and peppermint for anxiety and mental alertness. I don't believe that the benefits I am experiencing can be explained away by the placebo effect. I have noticed definite positive results.

I am learning how to use the strengths I still have and adjusting for my weaknesses. It is hard not to want to go at full speed, but there is nothing wrong with slowing down—I guess! Every day is different and symptoms may fluctuate in their severity, so I am finding solutions that will help compensate for my weaknesses. I've never been a very spontaneous person, and now even less so, since I could plan to do something, then wake up to find my symptoms have decided to get worse!

Suggested Prayer

Father God, forgive me for my self-reliance. Help me to always be obedient when You clearly show me the way. Help me to always have my eyes, ears, and heart open to the Holy Spirit's guidance and prompting. You are El Roi—the God Who Sees Me. (see Genesis 16:11–14, Psalm 139:7–12). I know that I can do all things through Christ,[4] all things work for my good,[5] and You are for me.[6] Please forgive me for the times I try to go my own way and miss what You want me to see or make a mess of my life. Thank You for Your faithfulness even when I am not. Help me to "lean not on my own understanding but in all ways acknowledge You.".[7] I love You, Lord, and want to glorify Your name through my life. In Jesus's name I pray, amen.

Personal Reflection

Do you have a chronic disease or know someone who has a chronic disease? What are your (or their) symptoms?

Are the symptoms all easily seen by others? Or do you have any invisible symptoms? Do you have a hard time explaining your symptoms to others?

Have you found a good resource for your questions beyond your doctor visits? What are those and how do they help you?

Do you have a good support group around you? If not, do you have 2 to 3 friends or family members that love and care about you that you can draw on in times of need? Would they feel blessed and honored that you asked them to be your support system? Would you feel blessed and honored if your roles were switched?

Have you experienced depression or anxiety over your or another's diagnosis? Are you receiving help from a clergy or counseling professional? If not, what are the reasons that you have not pursued that assistance? If so, how is this helping you?

What are some activities that you are no longer able to do? Do you feel embarrassed? What are some strategies you use to turn your weaknesses into strengths? Describe how it feels to make these changes in your activities of daily living.

Is there a strategy that I listed that could help you in your life? What would it be and how would it help you?

Write out a prayer that you would like to lift up to the Lord. Thank him for what he has done and ask for past hurts to be healed.

SHAKEN UP

Be strong and of good courage; do not be afraid,
nor be dismayed, for the Lord your God is
with you wherever you go. (Joshua 1:9)

Fear can be defined as an emotion caused by the belief that something is dangerous, likely to cause pain, or a threat. MS has shaken up my life and has caused me to believe that it, and the accompanying symptoms, is a threat to my well-being. The fear is what I struggle with the most. And I am angry I am fearful, because it is very unpleasant!

I am fearful:

- of stairs—especially when there are no railings. I have been taught how to use my cane, but I still freeze and feel immobilized when contemplating ascending or descending a set of stairs with no railing. I really am not safe in that environment. This is a side effect of my poor balance. As I move to step up or down, I feel very unstable.

- of inclines—I either trip up an incline or feel like I am falling when going down. I often get going too fast on a downward incline and have to stop and get my balance back. Whenever the surface is not flat (whether up or down or sideways), I feel out of control and off balance. I really have to concentrate on each step and take baby steps.

- of making it to the bathroom—although this has improved with medication.

- of appearing stupid as I struggle to find simple words. One day my daughter-in-law got out a game to play with my granddaughter called *Spot It*. It is a speed matching game that I could not do. During conversations I often cannot find the right words and finish my thoughts. Sometimes after the conversation is over I get the right word. Sometimes the word is just unable to be retrieved.

- of not being able to make it through the day because of overwhelming fatigue. I take a longer recovery time after any kind of exertion. I am exhausted after showering, doing my makeup, and getting dressed. It feels like I am ready for a nap. Usually by three o'clock in the afternoon I am done for the day. I can no longer complete a variety of shopping trips. Previously going to three to four stores was no big deal. I had lots of energy left over. Now I can maybe go to two to three, and that is if one is a drive through! Medication has helped but is not a panacea. Because of an insurance change I was in between medication to help with the fatigue when on a recent trip to Wal-Mart, then to Sam's Club, I was so fatigued that I seriously contemplated calling 911 for help getting out to my car. I sat on the tables in the food court for several minutes and ate one of the protein bars I had just bought and recovered enough to get to my car. But it was touch and go for a while.

- of walking farther than a block or two at a time. When walking that far, I use a cane, my leg starts to drag, and I have to use all of my concentration. I can't walk and talk or multitask! I have to make lots of stops. In grocery stores, I use the carts even when I am only buying one item. They are a great aid for balance and fatigue.

- of trying to change my hand dominance. This is definitely right-handed world! "Righty tighty lefty loosey" has a different meaning for those who are left handed.

- of cramps and spasms in my legs and feet. I take a medication for this too, and mostly it helps. Some nights I will endure hours of spasms and cramps, especially in the bottoms of my feet. I can be sitting quietly and my leg or foot will just suddenly jump and quiver. I can up the dosage of the medication when that happens, and generally that helps. As I mentioned above, the lavender essential oil has helped as well.

- of falling—always of falling. I have mentioned several issues previously. What is most frustrating is that I can be just standing and all of a sudden I will lose my balance and start swaying and feel out of control. I recently took an EEG that showed no seizure activity, which I was glad about!

- of my precarious balance. A funny thing happened recently. My bed is about eight inches away from the window. I was closing the window with one leg in between the window and bed. That was my right leg, and my left leg was on the bed. I was reaching to my right and putting weight on my right leg. And I started to lose the ability to stand on that leg, so I started slipping in between the bed and the wall. I tried to right myself several times, but I kept slipping further and further onto the floor. I was lying on my right side with my back against the wall and my front against the bed. My mother, who is eighty-nine, was not able to move the bed. So we had to call the fire department to come and move the bed and pick me up off the floor. I told them no social media pictures were allowed! If it wasn't so comical, it would be very tragic, especially if I was alone. I now know not to do that again!

Once diagnosed, I immersed myself in research and began going to a self-help group through the National Multiple Sclerosis Society (NMSS). I became a co-leader. I signed up for the weekly newsletter from MultipleSclerosis.net. I even wrote a couple of articles that were published in the newsletter. I recommend signing up for their weekly e-mail. I have met some lifelong friends who share this thing called MS. I learned that there was no cause and no cure, but I took a disease-modifying drug anyway.

According to the NMSS, there are several FDA-approved medications that have been shown to "modify" the course of MS by reducing the number of relapses and delaying progression of disability to some degree. In addition, many therapeutic and technological advances, as I have mentioned above, are helping us with MS manage symptoms. Advances in treating and understanding MS are made every year, and progress in research to find a cure is very encouraging.

I started taking an injectable medication but soon found that the side effects and the ability to find multiple injection sites (again, due to my weak right hand) was making it very difficult for me. I took one of the oral medications for about a year. Blood tests showed that my white blood cells were lower than they should be, so I have stopped the medication. My neurologist believes that I have transitioned into the secondary-progressive stage (my right hand is getting weaker and I am falling more), so for right now, I am no longer taking a disease-modifying treatment. No medication has been approved by the FDA for this stage, although there a lot of clinical trials attempting to find a medication.

I am still learning and attend local conferences and events when I can. I have volunteered for WalkMS in Washington and North Carolina. I still attend a self-help group and connect with others who share this insidious, horrible, unpredictable disease. However, it is too easy to become isolated.

On a recent visit back to Seattle, plans included going to Pike Street Market and going on a Duck Tour. The Ride the Ducks trips tour Seattle by land and water on a WWII amphibious landing craft. "It's a party on wheels that floats!"[1] Sounds fun, right? Well, I was convinced that I couldn't go. I thought about the intense walking, the sun and heat, climbing up and down the Duck, and how fatigued I would get. I was concerned about being a burden and slow everyone down. My son lobbied hard, and I decided to go. I am so, so glad I did! It was a great day. We stopped to rest several times and of course visited a Starbucks! The Ride the Ducks trip was awesome and lots of fun. I was definitely tired at the end of the day, but it was a wonderful reminder that I can still enjoy life, my family is here to support me, and I can "keep up" with more able-bodied people with a few simple adjustments, such as periodic rest periods.

All of the knowledge I have gained and the wonderful connections I have made have not decreased my fear. If anything, it has increased because of it. Fear can be a constant companion with panic and trepidation. However, there is light at the end of this tunnel—and back to fearlessness—and I am moving toward the Light. As I continue to study and apply God's word to my life, I am reminded of Psalm 119:105: "Your Word is a lamp to my feet and light to my path."

Suggested Prayer

Father God, I know that I am "Your workmanship created in Christ Jesus to do good works which You prepared beforehand that I should walk in."[2] I want to offer myself as a clean, smooth canvas, not worrying about what You choose to paint on it, and feel each stroke of Your brush. I know that You have not given me a spirit of fear, but of power, love, and a sound mind.[3] Like King David I cry out and say that my trouble has increased and I wonder if there is any help in You.[4] And also like David I say, "You have lifted up Your countenance upon me and put gladness in my heart.".[5] You are my "rock and fortress and my deliverer in whom I will trust.".[6] Your Son Jesus is the Light of the world, and because I follow Him I have the light of life.[7] I will walk as a child of light and find what is acceptable to You.[8] Lord Jesus, in You is the "light of men which shines in the darkness."[9] Help me, Lord, to always look toward Your light and not to my circumstances. I will fear (have awe of and reverence for) You because You are the "fountain of life and will turn me away from the snares of death."[10] In Jesus's name I pray these things. Amen.

Personal Reflection

What are some of the things that you are afraid of? Do you see fear as negatively impacting your life? What are some strategies that you use to overcome the fear you feel? Does your faith in God help you in anyway overcoming your fear?

Is isolation a problem for you? What can you do to live an active life? Are there support groups you can seek out?

Do a word search using a concordance or the Internet for "fear" in the Bible. I like using the BibleGateway.com. What have you found and how will this help you?

Write out a prayer that you would like to lift up to the Lord. Thank him for what he has done and ask him to remove your negative fears.

LIVING WELL

A time to weep, and a time to laugh, a time to mourn, and a time to dance. (Ecclesiastes 3:2)

The NMSS has wonderful resources, such as Live Well, Live Fully, Mood and Cognition, Positive Psychology, etc. I was fortunate to be a part of a clinical study through the Seattle Veteran's Administration Puget Sound Health Care System called Take Control of MS. We discussed subjects such as nutrition, exercise, and emotions. The 2015 summer/fall edition of *The Motivator*, published by the Multiple Sclerosis Association of America (MSAA), featured a series of articles on wellness in MS, impact of nutrition, exercise, and other strategies.

Let's first talk about exercise. NMSS, MSAA, and other MS organizations believe that exercise is vital to overall health. I couldn't agree more. I was a competitive swimmer growing up and through college. I love the sport and love the activity. Now, I swim three times a week, and it is *necessary* to my overall physical and mental health. I can swim twenty to twenty-five minutes and still have enough energy to shower, dry my hair, and drive home.

I like the showers at our fitness center. The showers are about four and a half feet square with hand rails on three sides. I can hold on with one hand and shampoo, condition, and rinse with the other. Using the hand rails allows me to close my eyes without falling over. Then, I keep my suit on while I use the blow dryer. If I would dress and then dry my hair, I would get too hot. And when I get overheated, my symptoms increase exponentially.

I was fortunate to receive assistance from the MSAA MRI Access Fund. I participated last year in SwimMS to give back and thank them for the help. If you are interested in donating to help others with MS and help fund research, both NMSS and MSAA are worthy organizations.

I used to love to walk. I would walk two to three miles several mornings each week. I could walk a mile in twelve to thirteen minutes. Now I use a recumbent cross trainer at least once a week. I have progressively increased speed and resistance. I never was a runner, so I simulate a walking speed (albeit slow—about sixty-five steps per minute). I can simulate walking a mile, which takes about thirty minutes, whereas outdoors I can barely do one-third of a mile without being totally wiped out. When I am outside and in difficult terrain, or have to walk long distances (one to two blocks) or in new surroundings, I use a cane and move very slowly, with lots of concentration.

Between the fatigue and the mobility issues, I feel like I have become very lazy. I have to pace myself and not do too much in one day. I need longer periods of rest and recovery in between activities. I plot out my weekly schedule with that in mind.

I have always loved to read and have over the years donated hundreds of books as I move to new locations (so I don't have to move them). Although reading is not physical exercise, it is a great leisure activity that I enjoy immensely. I have begun downloading on my tablet e-books from the library. I use the app OverDrive and set up an account with multiple libraries. These books are free, and you check them out similar to books in the library. You can have multiple books at a time and put a hold on books to receive them when they become available. It has saved me hundreds of dollars instead of buying the books. I still buy some because not all books are available in the e-book format. I also use a variety of puzzle apps and Lumosity brain games.

Over the past three years I have gone to a couple of great Physical and Occupational Therapists. I have a home program that I do almost every day. I volunteer at the Billy Graham Training Center in Asheville, North Carolina. I stay connected with people by joining activities and trips offered at the senior living facility where I am now living. So between physical exercise and keeping my mind sharp, I stay pretty active. But compared to my life before MS, I still feel like a couch potato, especially since I am no longer working.

Speaking of potatoes, I have begun watching my nutrition and how it affects my health. NMSS and others have noticed that the "white foods" (sugar, processed flour, white potatoes) increase inflammation and fatigue. If you want to know more go to: http://therealtruthaboutsugar.com/118/sugar-and-metabolism-2/. So I try to be very careful. I eat 85 percent dark chocolate (it is an acquired taste). But I do love ice cream! I try to limit sugar and usually don't eat any after midday. This is so I can metabolize it before bedtime. Otherwise, it seems to cause increased spasms and cramping. I love Pinot Noir wine, but as you may know, it reacts negatively with medications, so I limit that quite a bit as well. I also feel better if I go gluten free or at least find low glycemic foods. I don't eat white bread at all and try to find sprouted grains for breads. Sprouted grain bread uses the whole grain, is low glycemic, is easier to digest, and has a higher vitamin count when compared to other breads. I have also increased my fruits and vegetables.

It may sound like I have it all together. But I have my moments where I eat all the wrong things. I just try to be careful and understand the consequences. If I eat a lot of the "white foods" in any given day, the spasms and cramping increase in my legs and feet.

There has been a lot of studies trying to find out if there is an "MS diet." Everything I have read states that basic good nutrition is the best, such as low sugar and fat, high fiber, increasing fruits and vegetables (eating the rainbow), and decreasing red meats and processed foods.

Exercise and nutrition are a necessary part of my ability to maintain optimal health. However, it is my faith that keeps me on the right path. In the recently published *Wellness Toolkit for Self-Help Groups* by NMSS, it states that a dimension of wellness is spirituality. Spirituality is defined as developing positive relationships that nurture interconnectedness and active engagement in these relationships. It goes on to state the NMSS is committed to connecting people to resources we need for wellness. My self-help group is one such resource. The toolkit has discussion topics of all six wellness dimensions (physical, emotional, occupational, spiritual, social, and intellectual). The spiritual topic covers peace, purpose, kindness, engagement, and open discussions. One of the suggested guest speakers listed is a leader in the religious community. I am ecstatic that the NMSS is acknowledging the need for spiritual wellness. This toolkit is a great resource and I encourage self-help leaders to take advantage of it in their meetings. I know I will.

When I was twelve or thirteen, I went through confirmation classes in our local Methodist church. In the Methodist church, when an infant is baptized, a "confirmation" class is then offered for children in the sixth grade. This is a time to confirm the decision to follow Jesus Christ as your Lord and Savior. I took that step very seriously and look back on that as a very significant event in my life. In my twenties and early thirties, I walked away from a consistent discipleship in my faith. I was never taught how to be a follower of Jesus. So I went my own way, just assuming that my own thoughts and actions would be blessed by God since I was a

Christian. I always believed in Jesus Christ as my Savior. What I didn't understand was how to make Him Lord of my life as well.

Many of the above-mentioned MS wellness programs discuss grief and how we deal with it. Grief is a funny thing. According to Wikipedia, "grief is a multifaceted response to loss, particularly to the loss of someone or something that has died, to which a bond or affection was formed. Although conventionally focused on the emotional response to loss, it also has physical, cognitive, behavioral, social, and philosophical dimensions."[1] The Kübler-Ross model lists five stages of grief: denial, anger, bargaining, depression, and acceptance.

So if it is a response to something that has died, I can relate my MS experience to that definition. I have definitely experienced something that has died—my health, independence, fearlessness, mobility, and confidence. I have to design my day with fatigue and mobility in mind. How many errands can I run and in which order will provide the best use of my limited energy? My overall sense of well-being and my sense of who I am have shifted to being someone who is now disabled. Of course, with my vast experience working with children and adults with special needs, I realize that only my mind can make me truly disabled.

My denial (the first stage of grief) came before the diagnosis as I was sure that my full health was just a therapy strategy away—whether it be physical/occupational therapy, chiropractic adjustments, or doing the right exercise. I have not experienced denial after the diagnosis because deep down I knew something was not right, and there is pretty clear scientific evidence that there are multiple lesions in my brain and spine.

I am definitely angry. I am mad that I cannot be as fearless as I once was. For the first two and a half years after my diagnosis, I would watch other people walk, run, play with my grandchildren, and do simple everyday tasks and think, *I used to be able to do that and now I can't.* It is the simplest things like getting dressed in the morning, getting on the floor, getting back up, running from room to room after my granddaughters, walking through the parking lot, and going into a store that cause me to feel sorry for myself. I felt like everyone can see how poorly I walk and thereby wonder what is wrong with me.

So although I was fearless and confident, I was beginning to succumb to the negative feelings of low self-worth. Things were crashing in on me, and I knew I had to draw upon a deeper well than just my own resources.

Suggested Prayer

Father, You have given me a "spirit of wisdom and revelation in the knowledge of you.".[2] Whether You roar like a lion,[3] boom like thunder,[4] or speak through Your still small voice,[5] I pray You will continue to teach me and guide me. Help me always to see You as "Lord of lords and King of kings."[6] Thank You that You have given me the ability to still enjoy exercise of the mind and body. Soften my heart so I may I give You all the glory, honor, and praise. You are Jehovah Nissi, You are my banner, and that banner over me is love.[7] "Search me, O God, and know my heart; try me, and know my anxieties; and see if there is any wicked way in me, and lead me in the way everlasting."[8] In Jesus's name I pray, amen.

Personal Reflection

If you live with a chronic disease, or know someone who does, or you just want to be healthy, what are some healthy strategies you are using?

How often do you exercise and what is the intensity? Do you feel like you could do more? If so, what would that be?

Describe your other leisure time activities. Such as volunteering, reading, card games, video games, boardgames.

Have you received help from a physical therapist and/or occupational therapist? What kind of routine did they recommend? Are you still doing the exercises you learned? Why or why not?

We live in a world of fast food, packaged dinners, ready-made foods, and bulk sizes. What does your daily food intake look like?

I've heard it said that we should eat the rainbow. Which means fresh fruit and vegetables, lean meats, and whole-grain breads.

Are there some changes you can make in your daily diet to line up with that strategy? What would those changes be?

If you or someone you know has a chronic disease, are there suggestions and guidelines from the medical community you can follow? What are those? Are you following those now? Why or why not?

Do you consider yourself spiritual, what does that mean, do you pray, when and about what things? Do you have a church that you belong to? How did you choose it and why?

Did you go to church in your childhood? Would you consider your parents spiritual? Why or why not?

Do you attend church regularly? Why or why not? If you attend church what do you receive from going? Are you involved in any volunteering at your church? Why or why not.

What does having faith mean to you? Do you share your faith in anyway with others? Take some time and list all the ways God has blessed you.

What causes you to grieve? How do you work through the process? Do you feel your grief has negatively impact your life? Describe what your grief looks like.

Write out a prayer that you would like to lift up to the Lord. Thank him for what he has done and ask Him for wisdom and discernment as you make healthy life choices.

LIFE ABUNDANT

And the grace of our Lord was exceedingly abundant,
with faith and love which are in Christ Jesus. (1 Timothy 1:14)

Jesus says: "I have come that they may have life, and that they may have it more abundantly."[1] Paul states in Philippians 2:12, "Work out your own salvation with fear and trembling." I know I have been called to a life abundant. I also know that it takes a lot of fear and trembling. Does that seem contradictory? Well consider my life story.

Many environmental forces helped shaped my development. I grew up with role models such as June Cleaver, Donne Reed, Aunt Bee, Carol Brady, and Laura Petrie. My future mandated being a perfect wife and a mother. If you have ever seen Julia Roberts in the 2003 movie, *Mona Lisa Smile*, you can understand the era into which I was born. My pioneering, fearless spirit was cultivated through scouting and TV programs such as *Gunsmoke*, *Bonanza*, *The Avengers,* and *Rawhide.*

I am the middle child between two boys. There is a lot of fact in birth order psychology. My older brother was the honored firstborn son. My younger brother was the baby and got all the attention. I was the "forgotten" child. My opinions were not valued or cherished. So I learned to manipulate my surroundings and felt I had to be perfect to get noticed. Many middle children rebel to get attention. I went the other way. I wanted to get perfect grades and be successful in sports. I was the peacemaker. I am fiercely independent, a natural leader, and less dependent upon a relationship with my parents.

I was also the only granddaughter in the family, so I got special treatment from my grandparents. Each year in August, I got to spend a week with my grandparents (without my brothers!). My grandmother took me to downtown Columbus, Ohio, on the street car to shop for a whole new wardrobe for the coming school year.

I was protected as the "weaker sex"; girls were not supposed to be tough and ambitious. On a road trip when I was about eight, I remember teasing my brothers mercilessly, so they started hitting me. I started crying, saying that the boys were mean to me. They got punished; I didn't. Since I was not held accountable in this and other circumstances, I learned that manipulation brought me power. I really didn't get through this destructive way of thinking until I read the book *The Art of Leadership* by Max DuPree. The concept of "servant leadership" with Jesus as my model was new to me and life changing.

When I went to college, I wanted to continue to attend church. Since I was raised in the Methodist church, I thought I was a Methodist so had to attend a Methodist church. At this time in my life I knew nothing about the Holy Spirit and how He guides me. ("Now when they had gone through Phrygia and the region of Galatia, they were forbidden by the Holy Spirit to preach the word in Asia. After they had come to Mysia, they tried to go into Bithynia, but the Spirit did not permit them."[2]) When I went to the Methodist church in my college town, I felt an oppressive darkness. I didn't know what that was all about but knew I didn't want it. So to my young, naïve mind, I figured that I could not go to church since the Methodist church was not where I wanted to be. So I walked away from organized religion and lost my way for several years.

Even though I walked away, God did not. "For He Himself has said, 'I will never leave you nor forsake you.'"[3]

I joined a sorority and enjoyed the college party life. I still needed to be perfect, so my grades, succeeding on the swimming team, and goals of being a teacher were still paramount in my mind. I also knew that being a wife and a mother was something I had to achieve (a Mrs. Degree). I met a tall, dark, handsome man from India. He was a Hindu, and since I was not active in a church and therefore had no spiritual guidance, I didn't think it mattered. He could be a Hindu and I could be a Christian. I did not understand 2 Corinthians 6:14: "Do not be unequally yoked together with unbelievers. For what fellowship has righteousness with lawlessness? And what communion has light with darkness?"

We married, graduated, and started the adult life of working and making a family. After my kids were born, I started to realize that I needed to begin teaching them about God. I had learned enough about Hinduism that I knew that I didn't want my children to grow up believing in that religion. The kids and I started going to a Vineyard Fellowship Church. I immersed myself in Bible studies and home fellowship groups. I taught Sunday school and had a lot of fun doing so. One morning we were felling the walls of Jericho, and I was asked by an assistant pastor to quiet down as we were disturbing the service! Oops! (See Joshua 6:4–5.)

My husband and I were drinking fairly regularly during our first years of marriage. When I became pregnant and then a breast-feeding mom, I quit drinking. My husband, on the other hand, was quickly becoming an alcoholic. He was also a smoker. At age thirty-eight he had open heart bypass surgery, and subsequently after not adhering to a good recovery program, he committed suicide. I was suddenly a single mom with young children. The night of his death, I was lying in bed with my kids close and cried out to God, "Now what?" He told me He would be with me through it all. "For He Himself has said, 'I will never leave you nor forsake you.'"[4] A peace came over me that was unexplainable. "And the peace of God, which surpasses all understanding, will guard your hearts and minds through Christ Jesus."[5]

I didn't have time to dwell on the grief; I had to be the provider and both parents. I knew I needed support from my church family. In God's infinite wisdom, He brought me back to church before I knew I needed it. "And let us consider one another in order to stir up love and good works, not forsaking the assembling of ourselves together, as is the manner of some, but exhorting one another, and so much the more as you see the Day approaching."⁶

I had begun teaching physical education to students with mental disabilities. Through that work, I began a Special Olympics (SO) local organization through my school district. I grew to love SO and the work they did. I wanted to work for SO fulltime, so I went back to school, received an advanced degree, and began seeking sports and training positions throughout the country. I applied to a job in Montana and was chosen as the Director of Sports and Training for Special Olympics Montana.

My move to Montana reminded me of Abraham. Genesis 12:1 states, "Now the LORD had said to Abram: 'Get out of your country, From your family And from your father's house, To a land that I will show you.'" I did not know anyone in Montana, was starting a new job, and was taking my children away from friends and making them start new schools. My pioneering spirit was excited and energized. I am not so sure the kids felt the same way. Looking back, we should have had open and honest communication about the move and their feelings about it. Since I did not have a close relationship with my parents, I didn't understand how I could have that with my children.

And yet God does not look at me (and my past) without seeing the work of Christ on the cross. "But you are a chosen generation, a royal priesthood, a holy nation, His own special people, that you may proclaim the praises of Him who called you out of darkness into His marvelous light."[7] "There is therefore now no condemnation to those who are in Christ Jesus, who do not walk according to the flesh, but according to the Spirit."[8]

I had a lot of prayer leading up to and surrounding my decision, so I thought God was blessing *all* my decisions. Shortly after arriving in Montana, I needed some work done in the house I bought. My realtor suggested a friend of his that could do the work. He was tall, good-looking, and very much a "man's man." He began to court me very seriously. Although he had previously been to prison, I saw a repentant and changed man who loved God. I saw a man who was tender and loving to his sons. I saw what he wanted me to see.

Soon thereafter we were married. Again, there was a lot of prayer leading up to and surrounding my decision by myself and others. I hate to admit it now, and it is very hard to do so, but there were signs that this was a wrong decision, but I chose not to see them for what they were. I wanted to be married (still stuck in that '50s mentality that a woman's worth came through a husband) and have a dad for my kids. As it turned out, I was blinded. He was a wolf in sheep's clothing. What I forgot was to "Test all things; hold fast what is good."[9]

He had great hopes and dreams for a possibly very successful business. I brought some money to the table to assist him to set up this business. We were going to a great church, going to Bible studies, taking classes and considering leadership positions, and making wonderful friends. However, he squandered the money, failed at his business, and revealed that his belief system was not the same as mine. We went to several counseling sessions as I attempted to save the marriage. I was concerned about jumping into a divorce as I believe that God hates divorce.

"For the LORD God of Israel says that He hates divorce, for it covers one's garment with violence,' Says the LORD of hosts. 'Therefore take heed to your spirit, that you do not deal treacherously [with the wife of your youth]."'[10]

My husband's desire was to stay as he was and not fight for our marriage. Along the way, my children were ignored, and I did not raise them with the godly example I so very much wanted to. Our divorce was final in March 2003. I felt like I had died emotionally and spiritually along the way. I had only one place to find comfort and help. "Take My yoke upon you and learn from Me, for I am gentle and lowly in heart, and you will find rest for your souls. For My yoke *is* easy and My burden is light."'[11]

Throughout all of my trials, tribulations, fear, and trembling, I never lost sight of God. He has been my constant companion, even when I made erroneous life-changing decisions. "But the Helper, the Holy Spirit, whom the Father will send in My name, He will teach you all things, and bring to your remembrance all things that I said to you. Peace I leave with you, My peace I give to you; not as the world gives do I give to you. Let not your heart be troubled, neither let it be afraid."[12]

I continued going to my church, teaching Sunday school, and going to Bible studies. One in particular had a profound effect on me—*Experiencing God* by Henry Blackaby. I learned about something called crisis of belief. It is when God invites you into some new truth. The first crisis will be one of personal belief— what do I believe? The second is one of tension between old patterns and new options, and during the last crisis comes in the temptation to fall back into those old patterns. This concept literally changed my life.

In this you greatly rejoice, though now for a little while, if need be, you have been grieved by various trials, that the genuineness of your faith, being much more precious than gold that perishes, though it is tested by fire, may be found to praise, honor, and glory at the revelation of Jesus Christ, whom having not seen you love. Though now you do not see Him, yet believing, you rejoice with joy inexpressible and full of glory, receiving the end of your faith—the salvation of your souls.[13]

After my granddaughter was born in the Seattle area in 2006, I prayed fervently for direction. God led me to move to be close to my son and his family. My daughter was finishing up her Master's Degree and decided to also move to Washington. It was a great decision. We had many, many wonderful times. Eventually, my son and his wife had a second granddaughter.

Alcoholism is an insidious, generational disease. My son was swept away not only through his love of alcohol but prescription drugs as well. He was approximately three years clean and sober and seemed to be on a very good path. With alcoholism you never know when it might rear its ugly head. He recently relapsed but he is plugged into going to Alcoholics Anonymous meetings with a good sponsor. Leading up to his recovery four years ago was a very difficult time. He almost died a couple of times, was hospitalized several times, went through a twenty-eight days in-patient treatment twice, and along the way lost his marriage. He has since found and married a wonderful lady also in the AA program. God has had His hand on my son's life. He has brought him from the brink many times and set his feet on dry ground. "He also brought me up out of a horrible pit, Out of the miry clay, And set my feet upon a rock, And established my steps."[14] "Yea, though I walk through the valley of the shadow of death, I will fear no evil; For You are with me; Your rod and Your staff, they comfort me."[15]

My daughter has found a job in the Seattle area at which she is thriving. It is not in her area of education, but I guess that is the case for a lot of young professionals. Growing up my son and I bonded over several sports, especially football—yeah to the Super Bowl winners Denver Broncos! But my daughter never got the sports gene. Or so it seemed. For the last several years she has been rowing crew out of the Lake Washington Rowing Club. In her own words, "During the race the most important thing is to row together, to be one, a well-oiled machine working together to move the boat. As long as we are all together, we will have a good race. Rowing really is the epitome of a team sport. If one person is off, the whole boat is off.

"We row on one of the most famous strips of rowing water in the Pacific Northwest—the Montlake Cut. We are blessed with beautiful views of the Seattle skyline on Lake Union. Rowing has helped me to be stronger physically and mentally. It has made me be part of a team and understand what that truly means.

'My rowing club has been rowing on the waters of Washington since 1957 and has produced an Olympic rowing team—1960 Olympics. Stan Pocock (the son of George Pocock) helped start my club, along with Frank Cunningham. Stan was the first coach at Lake Washington Rowing Club! We row in Pocock rowing shells with pride. The current owner and operator of Pocock rowing shells (the oldest manufacturer of racing shells in the world!) continues to coach at our club as well."

I am so proud of my children. Their lives have not been a nice smooth existence. However, God has been faithful! Many years ago, a beautiful sister in the Lord gave me the following Scripture for my children. I pray it often and fervently! "I will pour water on him who is thirsty, and floods on the dry ground; I will pour My Spirit on your descendants, and My blessing on your offspring; they will spring up among the grass like willows by the watercourses."[16]

God continues to lead me, and I continue to learn more of His character and become more attuned to His voice. It is only then when I can truly live a life abundant. "And when he brings out his own sheep, he goes before them; and the sheep follow him, for they know his voice."[17] I love the book of Ephesians and pray often this prayer of Paul's:

> That the God of our Lord Jesus Christ, the Father of glory, may give to you the spirit of wisdom and revelation in the knowledge of Him, the eyes of your understanding being enlightened; that you may know what is the hope of His calling, what are the riches of the glory of His inheritance in the saints, and what is the exceeding greatness of His power toward us who believe, according to the working of His mighty power which He worked in Christ when He raised Him from the dead and seated Him at His right hand in the heavenly places, far above all principality and power and might and dominion, and every name that is named, not only in this age but also in that which is to come.[18]

I want to increase my knowledge of Him, His character, His great and awesome grace and mercy, and His amazing love and faithfulness.

My father's health was declining around the time I was laid off from work and seriously trying to find work in the Seattle area. But God said to go to North Carolina. I really didn't want to. Again and again, I try to be that independent person and go my own way. Again and again, God tried to lead me in His way. "Trust in the LORD with all your heart, and lean not on your own understanding; in all your ways acknowledge Him, and He shall direct your paths."[19] I moved to North Carolina in time to have a great few months with my dad before he passed away. Now I am trying to honor him and my mom by continuing to be present and available for all of my mom's needs. "Honor your father and your mother, that your days may be long upon the land which the LORD your God is giving you."[20]

******

There are two wonderful examples of womanhood in the book of Luke in the Bible. Martha and Mary were sisters. Their brother was Lazarus, who was raised from the dead after four days by Jesus (see John 11). In this context, Jesus is in their home for a meal. Martha is busy in the kitchen. Mary is sitting at Jesus's feet listening to every word He says. Martha goes to Jesus to complain that she is doing all the work. "But Martha was distracted with much serving, and she approached Him and said, 'Lord, do You not care that my sister has left me to serve alone? Therefore tell her to help me.'"[21]

Martha is type A who lives to work and works to live. I am a type A—full speed ahead, going my own way, fearless in my own strength, making decisions that I think are right, and forgetting God along the way. But He is faithful. He is quick to forgive. He never leaves me and is always ready to restore our relationship. He gives grace and mercy when justice is deserved. Let me say that again—He gives grace and mercy when justice is deserved. "For thus says the High and Lofty One Who inhabits eternity, whose name is Holy: 'I dwell in the high and holy place, With him who has a contrite and humble spirit, To revive the spirit of the humble, And to revive the heart of the contrite ones.'"[22]

You'll notice that I must come to Him with humility and with a contrite heart. He told Martha that Mary had chosen the right thing. "And Jesus answered and said to her, 'Martha, Martha, you are worried and troubled about many things. But one thing is needed, and Mary has chosen that good part, which will not be taken away from her.'"[23] Mary loves to worship the Lord and stay by His side.

Martha was driven by duty, and Mary was driven by relationships. I want to be more like Mary; and with God's help I can be as I turn to Him in humility and ask for the Holy Spirit's help.

> Nevertheless when one turns to the Lord, the veil is taken away. Now the Lord is the Spirit; and where the Spirit of the Lord is, there is liberty. But we all, with unveiled face, beholding as in a mirror the glory of the Lord, are being transformed into the same image from glory to glory, just as by the Spirit of the Lord."[24]

I love the story of David in the Bible. He has been described as a man after God's heart. "And when he had removed him, he raised up David to be their king, of whom he testified and said, 'I have found in David the son of Jesse a man after my heart, who will do all my will.'"²⁵ He was a teenage shepherd boy who went up against a Philistine "war machine" called Goliath with five stones and a slingshot. (1 Samuel 17.) Goliath was known to be nine feet, nine inches tall and carry about 200 to 210 pounds of armor. He was literally a scary dude coming up against the Israeli army. But David said, "You come to me with sword and spear and with the javelin but I come to you in the name of the Lord of hosts the God of the armies of Israel, whom you have defied. This day the Lord will deliver you into my hand and I will strike you and take your head from you. Then all the assembly shall know that the Lord does not save with sword and spear, for the battle is the Lord's, and he will give you into our hands."²⁶ He swung his slingshot and felled the giant!

David was anointed to be king by the prophet Samuel. Before he was able to move into being king, he was pursued relentlessly by the current jealous, crazy king who was removed from his reign due to his disobedience to God.

David was a murderer and adulterer. But he was also quick to admit his sins and return to God. Nathan was a trusted advisor to David. After David's affair with Bathsheba, Nathan came to him and told him a parable about a rich man who had no compassion for others. (See 2 Samuel 12.) David said that the offender should die. Nathan told him that he was that man. "So David said to Nathan, 'I have sinned against the LORD.' And Nathan said to David, 'The LORD also has put away your sin; you shall not die. However, because by this deed you have given great occasion to the enemies of the LORD to blaspheme, the child also who is born to you shall surely die.'"²⁷

David had to live with the consequence of his sin. "Do not be deceived, God is not mocked; for whatever a man sows, that he will also reap. For he who sows to his flesh will of the flesh reap corruption, but he who sows to the Spirit will of the Spirit reap everlasting life."[28] But his lineage brought about the greatest gift to humankind—Jesus. "His name shall endure forever; His name shall continue as long as the sun. And men shall be blessed in Him; All nations shall call Him blessed. Blessed be the Lord God, the God of Israel, Who only does wondrous things!
And blessed be His glorious name forever! And let the whole earth be filled with His glory.
Amen and Amen."[29]

David was a great and mighty king and warrior. He was also a psalmist—a musician writing poetry and worshiping the Lord through his music and instruments. And this is how he truly found the heart of God and was known as a man after God's own heart. David poured out his heart in songs and showed sincere and pure trust in the Lord. He made supplications to God, asked for good advice, even prayed for judgment on his enemies. He spoke about his history through the Psalms such as his exile, persecution, struggles, and the eventual triumph. David's seventy-four-plus songs continue to challenge, comfort, and inspire us three thousand years later.

It is through the Psalms that I have learned to cry out to God through thick and thin; return to Him when I go my own way; lean on His provisions and strength; let His Word be my light and lamp for the journey; and reveal my anger, depression, fears, and unending questions. He is a big God—He can take it. And I have learned more about who God is through the Psalms. He is omniscient, omnipresent, my creator, my shepherd, and my strength. And above all he is a caring Daddy. "He shall cry to Me, 'You are my Father, My God, and the rock of my salvation.'"[30]

Consider also the following verses. "You did not receive the spirit of bondage again to fear, but you received the Spirit of adoption by him we cry out, the Abba Father."[31] "And because you are sons, God is sent forth the Spirit of His son into our hearts, crying out, 'Abba, Father!' Therefore you are no longer a slave but s son, and if a son, then an heir of God through Christ.".[32]

******

Back to MS. In the spring of 2015, I started giving thanks to God that there are so many things I can still do beyond the disabling issues with which I deal. It was not an easy transition, but once I made it, I felt very free. How did I come to that breakthrough? Lots of prayer and diving into God's Word. He says in Psalm 91:1–2, "He who dwells in the secret place of the Most High, Shall abide under the shadow of the Almighty. I will say of the LORD, 'He is my refuge and my fortress; My God, in Him I will trust.'"

I don't want to be a lukewarm Christian and be spit out of God's mouth (Rev. 3:16 says, "So then, because you are lukewarm, and neither cold nor hot, I will vomit you out of My mouth."). I want to be in all the way. I give Him my anger, and He changes it into joy. He says in Isaiah 61:3, "To console those who mourn in Zion, To give them beauty for ashes, The oil of joy for mourning, The garment of praise for the spirit of heaviness; That they may be called trees of righteousness, The planting of the LORD, that He may be glorified."

The third stage of grief is bargaining. I have never been one to bargain with God and give Him empty promises. I don't say, "If you heal me of the MS, I will do such and so." Do I believe He still does miracles? Absolutely. Do I believe He can heal me? Absolutely. Do I believe He will? I am waiting expectantly. Does it make a difference in my faith if He doesn't? Absolutely not. Because I know that His grace is sufficient for me, for His strength is made perfect in weakness.[33] He also says: "Yet in all these things we are more than conquerors through him who loved us. For I am persuaded neither death nor life, nor angels nor principalities nor powers nor things present nor things to come, and height nor height nor death, nor any other created thing, shall be able to separate us from the love of God which is in Christ Jesus our Lord."[34]

I have definitely experienced the fourth stage, depression. Right after my diagnosis, I went to see a counselor for three to four months. That was a good decision. We talked about how my depression was interfering with my sleep and waking moments. She helped me figure out who this new me was and being okay with it. I've heard it said that I need to love my brain! Now depression can still visit me at any given moment or day. Sometimes it is immediate, sometimes it takes a while, but I remember that He gives me beauty for ashes!

Once I allowed myself to remember that God is for me, still loves me, and will never leave or forsake me, I started the journey back to a joyful and peaceful life. I have helped others to see that joy and peace don't depend on circumstances (unlike happiness), and I needed to put my money where my mouth was! Daily reminders help keep me on track. I read the Bible each day, do a daily devotional, attend a Bible study, and love going to church to worship with likeminded believers.

Recently I began to experience lingering feelings of being disconnected with life. I didn't feel like I was depressed, but this disconnected feeling coupled with the fatigue began to open my eyes to the fact that I probably was depressed and needed some medical assistance. During a recent trip to Seattle for my granddaughter's ninth birthday party, I even had to make myself be interested in playing with them. That really brought those feelings into my consciousness. Since I had good experiences on an antidepressant before, I decided to go back on it. Although I might gain weight again, I know now to be careful and have learned how to modify my diet to maximize my health. So far, I am experiencing a good emotional response to the medication and am not gaining weight! Yeah!

The final stage of grief is acceptance. Grief is not linear, so we can experience any of the stages at any time and in varying degrees. But I will never accept MS! God's Word says I am healed and I am His temple of the Holy Spirit. These are some of my favorites scriptures concerning these topics, but I challenge you to do your own study and research. I like using https://www.biblegateway.com.

- Job 33:24–26: "Then He is gracious to him, and says, 'Deliver him from going down to the Pit; I have found a ransom'; His flesh shall be young like a child's, He shall return to the days of his youth. He shall pray to God, and He will delight in him, He shall see His face with joy, For He restores to man His righteousness."
- Psalm 107:20: "He sent His word and healed them, And delivered them from their destructions."
- Isaiah 53:5: "But He was wounded for our transgressions, He was bruised for our iniquities; The chastisement for

our peace was upon Him, And by His stripes we are healed."

- Isaiah 58:8: "Then your light shall break forth like the morning, Your healing shall spring forth speedily, and your righteousness shall go before you; the glory of the LORD shall be your rear guard."
- Isaiah 40:31: "But those who wait on the LORD shall renew their strength; they shall mount up with wings like eagles, they shall run and not be weary, they shall walk and not faint."
- Luke 8:48: "And He said to her, 'Daughter, be of good cheer; your faith has made you well, go in peace.'"
- Luke 9:11: "But when the multitudes knew it, they followed Him; and He received them and spoke to them about the kingdom of God, and healed those who had need of healing."
- 1 Corinthians 3:16: "Do you not know you are the temple of God and that is the Spirit of God dwells in you?"
- 1 Corinthians 6:19: "Or do you not know that your body is the temple of the Holy Spirit who is in you, whom you have heard from God, and you are not your own?"

I feel that if I accept MS, I am denying His Word. It also means that I could deny that the robust research going would ever find a cause and a cure. And there is a lot of research going on. Check out these websites:

http://www.nationalmssociety.org/Research
http://www.ectrims-congress.eu/2015/ectrims-2015.html#&panel1-1
http://www.msworld.org/news-events/news/
http://mymsaa.org/ms-research-update/

Thomas Malcolm Muggeridge (March 24, 1903–November 14, 1990), known as Malcolm Muggeridge, was a British journalist, author, media personality, and satirist. During World War II, he worked for the British government as a soldier and a spy. He has said, "Every happening, great and small, is a parable whereby God speaks to us, and the art of life is to get the message." [35]

Suggested Prayer

El Shaddai, You are the All-Sufficient One, the Lord God Almighty.[36] El Elyon, you are the Most High God.[37] I do not want to be "tossed to and fro carried about every wind of doctrine."[38] I want to say with David, "Lead me to the rock that is higher than I" and "some trust in chariots, and some in horses, but I will remember the name of the Lord my God."[39] I want the kind of faith that Paul talks about in 1 Peter 1:7: "That the genuineness of my faith, being much more precious than gold that parishes, though it is tested by fire, may be found to praise honor and glory at the revelation of Jesus Christ." "Therefore most gladly I will rather boast in my infirmities, that the power of Christ may rest upon me."[40] Because Lord Jesus, You tell me that "My grace is sufficient for you, for My strength is made perfect in weakness."[41] All I need is You. Jesus, You are my rock,[42] my redeemer,[43] my shield,[44] my hiding place,[45] my armor,[46] my fortress,[47] my Savior,[48] my intercessor,[49] my Lord,[50] my King,[51] my lamb,[52] my lion,[53] my friend,[54] my God,[55] my teacher,[56] my constant companion,[57] my all. May my faith continue to be strengthened as it is tested. "For a day in Your courts is better than a thousand. I would rather be a doorkeeper in the house of my God than dwell in the tents of wickedness."[58] Thank You that when I seek You, I will find You, when I search for You with all my heart.[59] In Your precious name, Jesus. Amen!

Personal Reflection

After you read Luke 11, describe how you are either a Martha or a Mary. Do you long to have characteristics of the other? What does that look like?

What battle are you facing today? Read David's confrontation with Goliath in 1 Samuel 17. Can you say with David that the battle is the Lord's? Why or why not?

If you are not ready to say that the battle is the Lord's, what could you do to move in that direction?

I challenge you to read a Psalm each day. David wrote about half of them, and even though he had much persecution and many struggles, he was not afraid to let God know exactly how he felt. Write a Psalm that tells God how you feel and what you would like for Him to do in your life. It doesn't have to rhyme or be ready for a Pulitzer Prize, just pour out your heart. God is big; He can handle it.

There is a lot of research that states that having a heart full of gratitude is healthy for your overall well-being. Every night before you go to bed list 3 to 5 things you're thankful for. Start by listing five here.

Have you, or do you, suffer from depression? Is it situational or is it chronic? Are you getting help? Are you afraid to admit it? I encourage you to get the best help available to you.

Do you know that God loves you? Do you know that He's not mad at you? Do you know that He is for you? That He is in your corner? That He has your back? Read Isaiah 52:12. What does that mean to you? Read that every morning before your feet hit the floor and see how your world will change.

I listed some of my favorite verses that have to do with healing and the Holy Spirit. Do your own research and see what you find. How did the verses help you, encourage you, and enable you to find victory?

Is there active and robust research being done in the area of a chronic disease you are concerned with? I encourage you to read it and stay abreast of what is happening. How does reading the research help you day-to-day?

Write out a prayer that you would like to lift up to the Lord. Thank him for what he has done. Use the Psalm you wrote as a starting point.

GOD'S LOVE

For God is love. (1 John 4:8)
No hope does not disappoint, because the love of
God has been poured out in our hearts by the Holy
Spirit who was given to us. (Romans 5:5)

In the introduction, I quoted John 3:16—"For God so loved the world." What exactly does that mean? Does our definition(s) of love help us understand that verse? I am pretty sure they don't. First Corinthians 13:2–8 is often considered the love chapter. It is used in many a marriage ceremony. It says:

> Though I have all faith, so that I could remove mountains, but have not love, I am nothing. Though I do bestow on my goods to feed the poor, and though I give my body to be burned, but have not love, it profits me nothing. Love suffers long and is kind; love does not envy; love does not parade itself, is not puffed up; does not behave rudely, does not seek its own, is not provoked, thinks no evil, does not rejoice in iniquity, but rejoices in the truth; bears all things, believes all things, hopes all things, and endures all things. Love never fails.

Do you love like that? I know that I don't.

But God does! God is always a gentleman; He does not force Himself upon us. We have free will so that we will come to Him under no duress. The book of James can be a tough epistle to read. He says what he means and means what he says. In his fourth chapter, he speaks against pride, worldliness, and judgmental attitudes. But he also says, "Draw near to God and He will draw near to you."[1] God's love is kind, is not rude, rejoices in the truth, and bears with us because "God has loved you with an everlasting love; He has drawn you with loving-kindness."[2]

In our language, love can be used in many ways. I love the shirt you're wearing. I love that paint color that's on your walls. I will love you forever and ever. That movie was great—I loved it. In

Greek there are three words for love. Eros is physical love, such as sexual desire. Philos is esteem and affection in our casual relationships, such as a friendship. Agape is based on a deliberate choice of the one who's loving rather than the worthiness of the one who is loved. This love is unconditional, giving, and selfless. It is a love for the long haul.

This kind of love rejoices in the blessings others receive. It does not involve pride or self-glory. It does not seek its own reward. This love sets aside our own plans and agendas for the good of another. Agape love is not easily angered, nor is oversensitive. This love is not short-tempered toward other people's words or actions. This love is not blind, so when we recognize problems and failures in others (or ourselves), we do not lose our faith in the possibilities of what they (or we) might become. This love never gives up, and it believes we can change our lives for the good. Agape love continues unabated to build up and encourage others. "Greater love has no one than this, then to lay down one's life for his friends."[3]

And this is how we know that God loves us. "By this we know love, because He laid down His life for us."[4]

How do we grow this kind of love within us? I think this is a good answer:

> Whatever things are true, whatever things are noble, whatever things are just, whatever things are pure, whatever things are lovely, whatever things are of good report, if there is any virtue and if there is anything praiseworthy—meditate on these things. The things what you learned and received and heard and saw in me (the apostle Paul), please do, and the peace of God will be with you.[5]

Not only did Jesus die for our sins, but He also made a way for us to enter into God's presence so that we can develop an agape love for Him and receive it from Him. "Therefore brethren, having boldness to enter the holiest by the blood of Jesus, by a new and living way which He consecrated for us, through the veil, that is, His flesh."[6] The earth trembled when our loving God placed the sins of the world on Jesus for you and me. If that is not love, I don't know what is! "And Jesus cried out again with a loud voice, and yielded up his spirit. Then behold, the veil of the temple was torn into from top to bottom, and the earth quaked, and the rocks were split."[7]

Before Jesus died, the Jewish custom was that once a year, a priest would go into the Holy of Holies (a specially designed room of the Jewish temple behind the altar separated by a very heavy, thick tapestry) and pray for the deliverance of the people from their sins.

But now we can enter into God's presence without a priest into the Holy of Holies and speak to God personally through our prayers. That is pretty amazing! I feel so humbled by Jesus's death, which allows me to enter into a personal relationship with the God of the universe.

When we love another person, we want to spend time with him/ her, we listen intently to the other, and we can experience his/her love for us. It is the same with God—we must spend time with Him, listen intently to His voice through His Word, and experience His love through the Holy Spirit. Any other relationship we enter into, or voice we listen to, or experiences that are not centered on God are counterfeit, even with our spouses and family members. When we love God fully, we can love others fully. When we have a right relationship with God, we can rely on His Word (Jesus[8]) and the power of the Holy Spirit[9] to guide us and empower us to love as He loves us.

In Mark 6:45–52, we see Jesus walking on the water toward the disciples, who were in a boat traveling to the other side of the water heading to Bethsaida. Let me take apart the scriptures:

- He made His disciples get into the boat (v. 45)
- He sent them away (v. 46)
- He saw them straining at rowing, for the wind was against them (v. 48)
- He came to them (v. 48)
- He talked to them (v. 50)
- He went into the boat (v. 51)
- The wind ceased (v. 51)

What a beautiful picture of His love. He sends me into the storm, sees my struggle, comes to me, talks to me, is in the circumstance with me, and the storm ceases. Perhaps my circumstance doesn't cease, but the storms in my thoughts and emotions cease when I allow Jesus to "come into the boat" with me. I don't know about you, but I long for Jesus to be with me through the struggles of life. His peace, joy, and love allow me a safe haven in the midst of the worst storms that come against me.

God's love doesn't make sense to our finite minds, especially when we feel like things are not going the way we think they should. I for one get very impatient and try to run ahead of God. But I know His delay or answering my prayers with a no is always for my best. "My son, do not despise the chastening of the Lord, Nor detest His correction, for whom the Lord loves He corrects, just as a father the son in whom he delights."[10]

Suggested Prayer

Father God, how can I ever thank You for Your love? How can I ever thank You for the sacrifice of Your Son? I can only offer myself as a living sacrifice, holy and acceptable to You.[11] You desire that I love You with all my heart, with all the understanding, with all my soul, and with all the strength, and to love my neighbor as myself, which is more than all the whole burnt offerings and sacrifices of old.[12] And "thanks be to You, who gives me victory through my Lord Jesus Christ."[13] You are El Shaddai, the God Almighty;[14] You are Elohim, Creator, Mighty, and Strong;[15] You are El Olam, the Everlasting God.[16] And yet You love me. It is too wonderful and amazing sometimes to comprehend. "Show your marvelous loving kindness by Your right hand, oh You who save those who trust in You from those who rise up against them. Keep me as the apple of Your eye; hide me under the shadow of your wings, from the wicked who oppress me, from the deadly enemies who surround me."[17] Father, You tell me that I should "glory in tribulations knowing that tribulations produce perseverance, perseverance, character, and character, hope. Your hope does not disappoint because Your love has been poured out in my heart by the Holy Spirit who was given to me."[18] I pray that "the words of my mouth and the meditation of my heart be acceptable in Your sight, O Lord, my strength and my Redeemer."[19] In Your Son's precious name, amen!

Personal Reflection

What do you think of when I say God loves you?

Read 1 Corinthians 13:2-8 and describe your reaction to what love is.

When do you draw near to God? Only in the hard times? Or do you also talk to Him during the good times? Do you feel God drawing near to you at the same time? Sometimes we can be too busy telling God what we want to hear what God tells us. I am definitely guilty of that. I encourage you to develop hearing ears, attuned to God's voice by waiting in His presence.

Read Philippians 4:8-9. How can you implement that in your life today?

How did Mark 6:45-52 speak to you?

Write a love letter to God.

GOING FORWARD

I will lift my eyes to the hills—from where comes
my help? My help comes from the Lord, Who
made heaven and earth. (Psalm 121:1–2)

I have heard it said that our lives are like a kaleidoscope. Each time a kaleidoscope turns, there is another beautiful picture of combinations of bright colors. And at the center there has to be light, because without light, the kaleidoscope would just be dark. Jesus is the center of my kaleidoscope, and my life revolves around Him. He is also a light that shines through the colors that make them beautiful. He says in John 8:12, "I am the Light of the world. He who follows me shall walk not walk in darkness, but have the light of life." In Matthew 5:16 Jesus says, "Let your light shine before men, that they may see your good works and glorify your father in heaven." So not only is Jesus my Light, but I am His light to others. Paul tells us, "For you were once darkness, but now you are light in the Lord. Walk as children of the light for the spirit is all goodness, righteousness, truth.".[1]

Life takes strange, yet beautiful, twists and turns—like each turn of the kaleidoscope. Whether it was dealing with a spouse that committed suicide, a divorce, a difficult relationship with a friend or family member, a job layoff and subsequent change, or being on unemployment, I have worked hard to maintain my optimism, strong faith, and "can do" attitude. I know that all things work for my good—if I will let them!! I may be diagnosed with MS, but that is not who I am. I am an intelligent, capable, and strong woman who has done incredible things and has an amazing life. I will continue to keep my eyes on God and His purposes for my life. I will adjust and be stronger for it. I am committed to seeing all the turns of my life through Jesus's eyes instead of mine.

> Therefore we also, since we are surrounded by so great a cloud of witnesses, let us lay aside every weight, and the sin which so easily ensnares us, and let us run with endurance the race that is set before us, looking unto Jesus, the author

and finisher of our faith, who for the joy that was set before Him endured the cross, despising the shame, and has sat down at the right hand of the throne of God."[2]

God has blessed me with many nuggets of wisdom along the way. I encourage you to do your own intensive Bible study concerning topics that are of interest to you. I wish I could impart everything I have learned along the way, but that would take several books! In James 1:5 we are told, "If any of you lacks wisdom, let him ask of God, who gives to all liberally and without reproach, and it will be given to him."

- Martin Luther (1483–1546), a German theologian, said, "Many things I have tried to grasp, and have lost. That which I have placed in God's hands I still have." I am still learning this!
- Max Lucado is one of my favorite Christian authors. I have read several of his books. He has a marvelous way to get into the emotion behind scriptures and bring them to life. I recommend him highly.
- Calvin Miller was a seminary professor, theologian, and best-selling Christian author. He said that we fear searching for who we are because we might not like who we find. I can relate to that. But that means we leave God out, too, because I do not exist apart from Him. If I want to find who I am, I have to know who God says I am. Paul stated, "That you put off, concerning your former conduct, the old man which grows corrupt according to the deceitful lusts, and be renewed in the spirit of your mind, and that you put on the new man which was created according to God, in true righteousness and holiness."[3]In Romans 8:16–18 we learn, "The Spirit Himself bears

witness with our spirit that we are children of God, and if children, then heirs—heirs of God and joint heirs with Christ, if indeed we suffer with Him, that we may also be glorified together. For I consider that the sufferings of this present time are not worthy to be compared with the glory which shall be revealed in us."

- I used to love to worry. It made me feel that I was doing something to change the situation. I felt that I was helping God by trying to figure out how to move forward. However, worry has never brightened my day. Jesus tells us "therefore do not worry, saying, what shall we eat? Or what shall we drink? Or what should we wear? For your heavenly Father knows you need all these things. But seek first the kingdom of God, and his righteousness, and all these things shall be added to you. Therefore do not worry about tomorrow, for tomorrow will worry about its own things. Sufficient for the day is its own trouble."[4]

- I led a Bible study for my church called *Purpose-Driven Life* by Rick Warren. He says, "The purpose of your life is far greater than your own personal fulfillment, peace of mind, or even your happiness. It's far greater than your family, your career, or even your wildest dreams and ambitions. If you want to know why you were placed on this planet, you must begin with God. You were born *by* his purpose and *for* his purpose."[5]

- Paul tells us in Ephesians 6 to put on the full armor of God. I have heard some Bible teachers say we should wake up each day and visualize putting on God's armor. I prefer to never take it off. I want to never be without His righteousness, the gospel of peace, the shield of faith, my salvation, His Word, and prayer for all the saints.

- Often when we read Isaiah 53:5 ("But He *was* wounded for our transgressions, He was bruised for our iniquities; the chastisement for our peace was upon Him, and by His stripes we are healed"), we zero in on our healing by His stripes. My pastor recently focused instead on "the chastisement for our peace was upon Him." That really resonated with me. When Jesus died on the cross, He took the punishment meant for us so we could have His peace. He tells us in John 14:27, "Peace I leave with you, My peace I give to you; not as the world gives do I give to you. Let not your heart be troubled, neither let it be afraid." I am so thankful and full of praise for Jesus for His sacrifice so I can have His peace.

- The world does not offer any peace. Watch the nightly news for five minutes, and you can lose your peace. When I accepted Jesus as my Lord and Savior, I was filled with the Holy Spirit. And the fruit of having the Holy Spirit in me is "love, joy, peace, longsuffering, kindness, goodness, faithfulness, gentleness, self-control. Against such there is no law."[6] That's the kind of peace, joy, and faith I have!!

- Oswald Chambers was an early twentieth-century Baptist evangelist and teacher from Scotland. He wrote a daily devotional called *My Utmost for His Highest*. I recommend it highly. It was my constant companion until it literally fell apart. He said that faith is believing God will always stand by us even when we don't understand.

- Romans 8:31, 39 says "If God is for us, who can be against us? ... nor any other created thing, shall be able to separate us from the love God which is in Christ Jesus our Lord." Remember, God is for you! *God* is for you. God *is* for you. God is *for* you. God is for *you*!

- I have ignored God's leading many times over the years and can say along with Paul, "Christ Jesus came into the world to save sinners, of whom I am chief."[7] But I can also say with Paul, "I have fought the good fight, I finished the race, I have kept the faith. Finally, there is laid up for me the crown of righteousness, which the Lord, the righteous judge, will give to me on that day, and not to me only but also to who also have loved his appearing."[8] And "we are hard-pressed on every side, yet not crushed; we are perplexed, but not in despair; persecuted, but not forsaken; struck down, but not destroyed."[9] So even though I am hard-pressed, perplexed, persecuted, and struck down, I am not crushed, in despair, forsaken, or destroyed! Amen!

- You *must* be your own advocate and not take what a doctor says at face value. They are not all knowing, with superhero powers! I have learned this the hard way!

- I have known people, my son included, who had to suffer through shingles. After a recent fall, I thought I had gotten rug burns on my back. It turned out to be shingles. This is a very interesting reaction to the stress of a bad fall, whereby my already compromised immune system reacted by developing shingles. As most people will tell you, shingles are not fun and can be very painful. My neurologist wants me to get the shingles immunization shot. I usually stay away from immunization shots because I so rarely get sick. My neurologist explained to me that to get the flu or shingles would be worse combined with the MS, so I have changed my way of thinking.

- My constant hope and prayer is that God will not leave me where I am but continue to teach and guide me. And in fact He loves me too much to allow that to happen.

He wants me to say with John the Baptist (see John 3:30), "Let Him increase and I decrease."

- There is a catch. I have to be obedient. Even Jesus had to be obedient to His Father. "Though He was a Son, yet He learned obedience by the things which He suffered. And having been perfected, He became the author of eternal salvation to all who obey Him."[10]
- Do I long for suffering in my life? Of course not. However, sometimes God uses trials and suffering to mold me more into His image. As you study the Bible, you will see a stark difference in the lives of those who submitted to God's leading and those who did not. We often hear of the "patience of Job." In reality, he wasn't all that patient, as he questioned God quite frequently. However, he learned obedience through his trials and suffering. He lost everything—wealth, possessions, and sons and daughters. His friends and wife wanted him to curse God and die. He refused. Instead He cried out to God in repentance and was restored. "Then Job answered the LORD and said: 'I know that You can do everything, And that no purpose of Yours can be withheld from You. You asked, 'Who is this who hides counsel without knowledge?' Therefore I have uttered what I did not understand, Things too wonderful for me, which I did not know. Listen, please, and let me speak; You said, 'I will question you, and you shall answer Me.' I have heard of You by the hearing of the ear, But now my eye sees You. Therefore I abhor myself, And repent in dust and ashes."[11]
- Many of you might be wondering how I know Jesus is alive. I know He lives because He lives in me through the power of the Holy Spirit. Please see:

- o Romans 5:1–5: "Therefore having been justified by faith, we have peace with God through our Lord Jesus Christ, through whom also we have access by faith into this grace in which we stand, and rejoice in the hope of the glory of God. And not only that, but we also glory in tribulations, knowing that tribulation produces perseverance; and perseverance, character; and character, hope. Now hope this not disappoint, because the love of God has been poured out in our hearts by the Holy Spirit who was given to us."
- o Romans 6:9–11: "knowing that Christ, having been raised from the dead, dies no more. Death no longer has dominion over him. For the death He died, He died to sin once for all; but the life that He lives, He lives to God. Likewise you also, reckon yourselves to be dead to sin, but alive to God in Christ Jesus our Lord."
- o 2 Corinthians 1:22: "He who establishes us with you in Christ and has anointed us in God, Who also has given us the Spirit in our hearts as a guarantee."
- o 2 Corinthians 13:3–5: "Since you seek approval of Christ speaking in me, who is not weak toward you, but mighty in you. For though He was crucified in weakness, He lives by the power of God. For we also are weak in Him, but we shall live with Him by the power of God toward you."
- o Ephesians 1:12–14: "that we who first trusted in Christ should be to the praise of His glory. In Him you also trusted, after you heard the word of truth, the gospel of your salvation; in whom also, having believed, you were sealed with the Holy Spirit of

promise, who is also a guarantee of our inheritance until the redemption of the purchased possessions, to the praise of his glory."

- o 2 Timothy 1:14: "That good thing which was committed to you, keep by the Holy Spirit who dwells in us."
- o John 14:16, 25–27: "If you love Me (Jesus), keep my Commandments. And I will pray the Father, and He will give you another Helper, that He may abide with you forever—the Spirit of truth. These things I've spoken to you while being present with you. But the Helper, the Holy Spirit, whom the Father will send in My name, He will teach you all things, and bring to your remembrance of things that I've said to you."
- o Luke 11:13: "If you then, being evil, know how to give good gifts to your children, how much more will your heavenly Father give the Holy Spirit to those who ask Him!"
- o 1 John 4:13: "By this we know that we abide in Him, and He in us, because He has given us of His Spirit."
- o 2 Peter 1:3: "His divine power has given to us all things that pertain to life and godliness, through the knowledge of Him who called us by glory and virtue."
- o Zechariah 4:6: "Not by might nor by power, but by my spirit"

- Not only is the Holy Spirit in me, but He is also about me. God has given me a picture of a glass submerged in water. Not only is there water in the glass, but it is all around the glass. There are many references in the Bible comparing the Holy Spirit to water and rivers of water. John 4:1–26 is the account of Jesus speaking to a Samaritan woman (the Jewish people in that day hated the Samaritans) at the local watering well where women gathered to get water for their households. Jesus told her He had water that, when drunk, will cause us to never be thirsty again. And this water will become a fountain of water rising up in us. In John 7:37–39, it states "On that last day, the great day of the feast[12], Jesus stood and cried out, saying 'If anyone thirsts, let him come to Me and drink. He who believes in Me, as the Scripture has said, out of his heart will flow rivers of living water.'"

- Dr. Neil T Anderson, Freedom in Christ Ministries, developed a beautiful list of Scriptures that has made a huge impact on my life. It is called Who I Am in Christ.[13] When I first found this through a Bible study, I spent time each day affirming those scriptures in my life. It was a time during the last days of my second marriage and right after the divorce. I needed to know I was accepted, secure, significant, and free from mistakes of the past. Although, I do not affirm those scriptures daily anymore, I often pick the list up during times of questioning God's presence in my life, and they become a lifeline back into His love.

- I mentioned at the beginning that I love praying God's Word and His names. Another Bible study I took was *Lord, I Want to Know You* by Kay Arthur, Precept Ministries International. I learned His names reveal His character. I want to know Him more, so His character is the best way to know Him. My constant prayer is "that the God of our Lord Jesus Christ, the Father of glory, may give to (me) the spirit of wisdom and revelation in the knowledge of Him."[14]

- You will find a sample of His names in the resource section. You can also do a simple Internet search to find more resources.

- The book of Ephesians is my favorite book in the Bible. There are such powerful prayers that Paul prayed for the Ephesians. Many of those have become prayers of mine for me and others. I have given myself a promise to commit the entire book to memory. I have not done so, but now that I have made it public, I better get on it!

- Horatio Spafford (1828–1888) was a wealthy Chicago lawyer. He had a beautiful home, a wife, four daughters, and a son. He was also a devout Christian and faithful student of the scriptures. Due to the 1871 Great Chicago fire (which damaged most of his real estate holdings), the economic downturn of 1873, and tragic deaths of all of his children, he wrote the hymn, "It Is Well with My Soul."[15] It is a wonderful example of overcoming tragedy and rising above our circumstances, through the death and resurrection of Jesus.

If anything I have said encourages you to draw closer to God, then I have succeeded. If you are not plugged into a church or small home group, I encourage you to do so. If you would like to learn more about how to have a personal relationship with Jesus and receive the Holy Spirit, I encourage you to go to http://peacewithgod.net or http://needhim.org. Developing a relationship with Jesus will be the best thing you ever did for yourself. It is a very simple process, and yet it is not easy.

We have to admit we are sinners, believe the work Jesus did on the cross, and confess our sins before our loving Daddy (who knows them already). You can pray the following prayer to accept Jesus as your Lord and Savior: "Dear Lord Jesus, I know I am a sinner, and I ask for your forgiveness. I believe you died for my sins and rose from the dead. I trust and follow you as my Lord and Savior. Guide my life and help me to do your will. In your name, Amen."[16]

It is my prayer that each of you have been ministered to by my journey back to fearlessness. I have prayed for each of you throughout the process of writing this book. I ask that you pray for me as well as we journey on this thing called life. "Now I beg you, brethren, through the Lord Jesus Christ, and through the love of the Spirit, that you strive together with me in prayers to God for me."[17]

I am fearless because I am "strong in the Lord
and in the power of His might."[18]
I have the world by the tail because "He that is in me is stronger
than he that is in the world."[19]
I know what I want and go after it because
I "seek first His kingdom"[20]
and I "know the voice of my Shepherd."[21]
I am successful and feel good about my life because
"the battle is the Lord's"[22] and I am "more than
a conqueror through Him who loves me."[23]
Praise God!

Suggested Prayer

Father God, You are the Alpha and the Omega, the beginning and the end.[24] "Every good and perfect gift comes from you, the Father of Lights."[25] Please forgive me when I try to operate in my own sense of self-sufficiency, my own wisdom, and try to figure out my own plan. Forgive me, Lord, for running ahead of You or slowing down and not keeping up with You. I desire to be clay in Your hand, for You are my Potter.[26] My desire is to be Your love letter to others written not with ink but Your Spirit and not on tablets but on the hearts of others.[27] I know that all things that pertain to life and godliness You have given me. You have given me "exceedingly great and precious promises."[28] All of your promises are "Yes and Amen."[29] I do not count myself as apprehended all of Your wonderful mysteries, but I pray for You to help me to forget those which are behind and reach forward to those things which are ahead.[30] My desire is to tremble at Your word.[31] My desire is that Your hope will fill me with "all joy and peace as I trust in you so that I may overflow with hope by the Holy Spirit."[32] My desire is to think about all things that are true and noble and just and pure and lovely and have a good report. I pray, Father, that if there is any virtue, anything praiseworthy, that I will meditate on these things.[33] I know that I am Your workmanship created in Christ Jesus to do the good works You create for me.[34] I know that I am established, anointed, and sealed in You.[35] Thank You that "no weapon formed against me will prosper."[36] I want to be so committed to Your will that I can say "be it to me according to your word."[37] I know that I "can do all things through Christ who strengthens me."[38] I have confidence that You will complete the good work You started in me.[39] May I "rejoice always and pray without ceasing by in everything giving thanks for that is Your will."[40] Now to "You, who is able to do exceedingly, abundantly above all that I can ask or think, be the glory to all generations forever and ever. Amen."[41]

Personal Reflection

Describe how the kaleidoscope of your life would look. Is it one continual beautiful picture or a series of broken pieces of glass? If you look at your kaleidoscope through the light of Jesus, how does that affect your vision as you look back and look forward?

Describe some words of wisdom that have affected you in positive ways. Try to come up with at least 5 to 7.

Are you a worrier? What does Jesus say about worry?

Read Ephesians 6:1-18. Do you have all of God's armor? What might you be missing? Or what do you forget you have? What can you do to stand powerful in God's armor?

Do you know Jesus is alive and you are the temple of the Holy Spirit? If not, please go to a trusted friend, Pastor, or family member to help you with these difficult yet amazing truths.

Did the "Who I am in Christ" resource help you? Is there someone else that you could give it to that it would bless? Who is that person and when will you make this gift available to them?

Have you made a meaningful decision after reading this book? What is that decision? Please email me and let me know. joannmaxwell@fearlessinJesusChrist.com.

Can you say with me my final words in the book (I am fearless.....)? Why or why not?

Write out a prayer that you would like to lift up to the Lord. Thank him for what he has done and ask Him to give you His prospective on your life.

REFERENCES

Who I Am In Christ

I Am Accepted
John 1:12 I am God's child.
John 15:15 I am Christ's friend.
Romans 5:1 I have been justified.
1 Corinthians 6:17 I am united with the
Lord, and I am one spirit with Him.
1 Corinthians 6:20 I have been bought
with a price. I belong to God.
1 Corinthians 12:27 I am a member of Christ's Body.
Ephesians 1:1 I am a saint.
Ephesians 1:5 I have been adopted as God's child.
Ephesians 2:18 I have direct access to
God through the Holy Spirit.
Colossians 1:14 I have been redeemed
and forgiven of all my sins.
Colossians 2:10 I am complete in Christ.

I Am Secure
Romans 8:1-2 I am free from condemnation.
Romans 8:28 I am assured all things work together for good.

Romans 8:31-34 I am free from any
condemning charges against me.
Romans 8:35-39 I cannot be separated from the love of God.
2 Corinthians 1:21-22 I have been established,
anointed and sealed by God.
Philippians 1:6 I am confident that the good work
God has begun in me will be perfected.
Philippians 3:20 I am a citizen of heaven.
Colossians 3:3 I am hidden with Christ in God.
2 Timothy 1:7 I have not been given a spirit of
fear, but of power, love and a sound mind.
Hebrews 4:16 I can find grace and mercy in time of need.
1 John 5:18 I am born of God and the
evil one cannot touch me.

I Am Significant
Matthew 5:13-14 I am the salt and light of the earth.
John 15:1,5 I am a branch of the true vine, a channel of His life.
John 15:16 I have been chosen and appointed to bear fruit.
Acts 1:8 I am a personal witness of Christ.
1 Corinthians 3:16 I am God's temple.
2 Corinthians 5:17-21 I am a minister of reconciliation for God.
2 Corinthians 6:1 I am God's coworker (see 1 Corinthians 3:9).
Ephesians 2:6 I am seated with Christ in the heavenly realm.
Ephesians 2:10 I am God's workmanship.
Ephesians 3:12 I may approach God
with freedom and confidence.
Philippians 4:13 I can do all things through
Christ who strengthens me.

A Sample of the Names of God from the Old Testament

El Shaddai	Lord God Almighty
El Elyon	The Most High God
Adonai	Lord, Master
Yahweh	Lord, Jehovah
Jehovah Nissi	The Lord My Banner
Jehovah Raah	The Lord My Shepherd
Jehovah Rapha	The Lord That Heals
Jehovah Shammah	The Lord Is There
Jehovah Tsidkenu	The Lord Our Righteousness
Jehovah Mekoddishken	The Lord Who Sanctifies You
El Olam	The Everlasting God
Elohim	God
Qanna	Jealous
Jehovah Jireh	The Lord Will Provide
Jehovah Shalom	The Lord Is Peace
Jehovah Sabaoth	The Lord Of Hosts

It Is Well with My Soul

When peace, like a river, attendeth my way,
When sorrows like sea billows roll;
Whatever my lot, Thou hast taught me to say,
It is well, it is well with my soul.

It is well (it is well),
with my soul (with my soul),
It is well, it is well with my soul.

Though Satan should buffet, though trials should come,
Let this blest assurance control,
That Christ hath regarded my helpless estate,
And hath shed His own blood for my soul.

It is well (it is well),
with my soul (with my soul),
It is well, it is well with my soul.

My sin, oh the bliss of this glorious thought!
My sin, not in part but the whole,
Is nailed to His cross, and I bear it no more,
Praise the Lord, praise the Lord, O my soul!

It is well (it is well),
with my soul (with my soul),
It is well, it is well with my soul.

For me, be it Christ, be it Christ hence to live:
If Jordan above me shall roll,
No pang shall be mine, for in death as in life
Thou wilt whisper Thy peace to my soul.

It is well (it is well),
with my soul (with my soul),
It is well, it is well with my soul.

And Lord haste the day, when my faith shall be sight,
The clouds be rolled back as a scroll;
The trump shall resound, and the Lord shall descend,
Even so, it is well with my soul.

It is well (it is well),
with my soul (with my soul),
It is well, it is well with my soul.

ACKNOWLEDGMENTS

Thank you first of all to Jesus, My Lord and Savior. Without Jesus as my constant companion and the Holy Spirit working through me, I would definitely be a wreck of a person.

Huge thanks to the staff at WestBow Press. You all made the process of getting this book published a joy!

Thank you to my good friend Donna Eakman, who has helped me with editing and also general feedback on the flow of this book. I appreciate all of your words of wisdom. Your friendship is forever, and I appreciate all the times that we have cried, laughed, and hiked in the mountains and the wonderful meals we've shared together. You are a forever friend.

Thank you to Cathy Young, who has also encouraged me greatly over the past few years. She is a good friend and one who will stand the test of time. Whenever I wonder whether my friends remember me, an e-mail comes over the digital airwaves from you with words I need to hear! Thank you also for all of the fun we had as we packed up my life and moved from Seattle to North Carolina. That will forever be in my memory. If you ever want to do another long-distance road trip, let me know!

Thank you to Pastor Rob Cuevas, pastor at Tabernacle of Praise in Fletcher, North Carolina. I appreciate your wisdom, your ability to make the scriptures come alive, your love, and your unparalleled leadership as my pastor.

Thank you also to Linda Moran, who wrote the foreword. We met because of our MS diagnosis and have forged a beautiful friendship. I appreciate your wisdom, your outlook on life, our discussions about our faith, and your encouragement for me to even begin writing this book. It is because of your encouragement and vision that this book is coming to life.

I want to especially thank my children. You are my joy, my inspiration, my trials, my achievement. I look to you and see that I did some things well.

NOTES

Introduction
1 2 Timothy 3:16-17
2 John 3:16-17
3 Matthew 6:9-10
4 John 7:17

Life before MS
1 Genesis 22:10-14
2 Revelation 4:11

Enter MS
1 (National Multiple Sclerosis Society http://www.nationalmssociety.org/ What-is-MS/Definition-of-MS, February, 26, 2016)
2 (National Multiple Sclerosis Society, http://www.nationalmssociety.org/ What-is-MS/Types-of-MS, February 26, 2016)
3 (National Multiple Sclerosis Society, http://www.nationalmssociety.org/ What-is-MS/What-Causes-MS, February, 26, 2016)
4 Philippians 4:13
5 Romans 8:28
6 Romans 8:31
7 Proverb 3:3-5

Shaken Up
1 Ride the Ducks of Seattle, http://www.ridetheducksofseattle.com, August, 15, 2015
2 Ephesians 2:10
3 1 Timothy 1:3

4 Psalm 3:1-2
5 Psalm 4:6-7
6 Psalm 18:2
7 John 8:12
8 Ephesians 5:8-10
9 John 1:4
10 Proverbs 14:27

Living Well
1 Wikipedia, the Free Encyclopedia, https://en.wikipedia.org/wiki/Grief, September 29, 2015
2 Ephesians 1:17
3 Amos 3:8
4 Revelation 8:5
5 1 Kings 19:12
6 Revelation 17:14
7 Song of Solomon 2:4
8 Psalm 139:23-24

Life Abundant
1 John 10:10
2 Acts 16:6-7
3 Hebrews 13:5
4 Hebrews 13:5
5 Philippians 4:7
6 Hebrews 10:24-25
7 1 Peter 1:9
8 Romans 8:1
9 Philippians 4:21
10 Malachi 2:16
11 Matthew 11:29-30
12 John 14:25-26
13 1 Peter 1:6-9
14 Psalm 40:2
15 Psalm 23:4
16 Isaiah 44:3-4
17 John 10:4
18 Ephesians 1:17-21

19 Proverbs 3:5-6
20 Exodus 20:12
21 Luke 10:40
22 Isaiah 57:15
23 Luke 10:41-42
24 2 Corinthians 3:16-18
25 Acts 13:22
26 1 Samuel 17:45-47
27 2 Samuel 12:13-14
28 Galatians 6:6-7
29 Psalm 72:17-19
30 Psalm 89:26
31 Romans 8:15
32 Galatians 4:6-7
33 2 Corinthians 12:9
34 Romans 8:37-39
35 (http://www.heartlight.org/cgi/quotemeal.cgi)
36 Genesis 17:1
37 Psalm 57:2
38 Ephesians 4:14
39 Psalm 61:2, 20:7
40 2 Corinthians 12:9
41 2 Corinthians 12:9
42 Psalm 31:3
43 Jeremiah 50:34
44 Psalm 28:7
45 Psalm 32:7
46 Ephesians 6:11
47 2 Samuel 22:2
48 Jude 25
49 Romans 8:26
50 Luke2:11
51 Revelation 19:16
52 John 1:29
53 Revelation 5:5
54 Matthew 11:19
55 Exodus 3:4
56 John 13:13
57 Zechariah 13:7

58 Psalm 84:10
59 Jeremiah 29:13

God's Love
1 James 4:8
2 Jeremiah 31:3
3 John 15:13
4 1 John 3:16
5 Philippians 4:8-9
6 Hebrews 10:19-20
7 Matthew 27:50-51
8 John 1:1
9 Galatians 5:22-23
10 Proverbs 3:11-12
11 Romans 12:1
12 Mark 12:33
13 1Corinthians 17:57
14 Genesis 49:24
15 Genesis 17:7
16 Psalm 91:1-3
17 Psalm 17:7-9
18 Romans 5:3-5
19 Psalm 19:14

Going Forward
1 Ephesians 5:7-9
2 Hebrews 12:1-2
3 Ephesians 4:22-24
4 Matthew 6:31-34
5 http://www.heartlight.org/cgi/quotemeal.cgi
6 Galatians 5:22-23
7 1 Timothy 1:15
8 2 Timothy4:7-8
9 2 Corinthians 4:8-9
10 Hebrews 5:8-9
11 Job 42:1-6
12 This feast was originally designed to celebrate the huts that Israelites lived in during their forty days in the desert after their exodus from Egypt.

Later it became known as a celebration of the harvest as it occurs at harvest time.

13 Neil T. Anderson, *Victory Over the Darkness*. (Grand Rapids, MI: Bethany House Publishers, 2000). "Used by Permission.

14 Ephesians 1:17

15 http://www.sharefaith.com/guide/Christian-Music/hymns-the-songs-and-the-stories/it-is-well-with-my-soul-the-song-and-the-story.html

16 http://peacewithgod.net

17 Romans 15:30

18 Ephesians 6:10

19 1 John 4:4

20 Matthew 6:33

21 John 10:16

22 1 Samuel 17:47

23 Romans 8:37

24 Revelation 20:16

25 James 1:17

26 see Jeremiah 18:6

27 see 2 Corinthians 3:3

28 2 Peter 1:3

29 2 Corinthians 1:20

30 Philippians 3:13

31 Isaiah 66:2

32 Romans 15:13

33 Philippians 4:8

34 Ephesians 2:10

35 2 Corinthians 2:1

36 Isaiah 54:17

37 Luke 1:38

38 Philippians 4:13

39 Philippians 1:4

40 Philippians 4:17-18

41 Ephesians 3:20

Printed in the United States
By Bookmasters